MW01519196

Some Were Paupers, Some Were Kings:
Dispatches from Kansas

Some Were Paupers, Some Were Kings:

Dispatches from Kansas

Mark E. McCormick

BLUE
CEDAR
PRESS

WICHITA

Some Were Paupers, Some Were Kings: *Dispatches from Kansas*

Copyright © 2017 by Mark E. McCormick. All rights reserved. No part of this book may be reproduced or utilized in any manner whatsoever without written permission, except in the case of brief quotations embodied in critical articles and reviews. Inquiries should be addressed to:

Blue Cedar Press
PO Box 48715
Wichita, KS 67201

First edition
10 9 8 7 6 5 4 3 2 1

ISBN: 978-0-9960970-7-9

Cover photo by Keisha Ezerendu.
Author photo by Diane Criner.
Composition by Caron Andregg, Sea Cliff Media Marketing.
Editor, Laura Tillem.

Columns are used with permission of *The Wichita Eagle* and "Whether You Like Ice-T or Not, It Happens" by permission of *The Louisville Courier-Journal*. "There for Us" and "Ali: Speaking to a Loss Shared by Many" used by permission of the Kansas Leadership Center's *The Journal*.
* Indicates an award-winning column.

Printed in the United States of America
at BookMobile, in Minneapolis, MN.

Dedication

I'm grateful to the incredible Blue Cedar Press Board for finding something worthy enough in my journalism work to warrant a book project. Thank you Laura Tillem for your editing and thank you Dr. Gretchen Eick, the Rev. Michael Poage, Dr. Crystal Coles and Abril Marshall for your work in assembling this book.

In addition to my family for whom my love knows no bounds, I'd like to dedicate this book to the following:

To my mother, Ethel Mae McCormick, for her selfless love and work ethic and to my father, Joseph Langston McCormick, Jr. for his storytelling, poems and relentless pride in our family and in me; my sister, Chandra Lynn McCormick who was the first journalist I ever knew and my professional inspiration; my brother, Joseph Langston McCormick, IV, who inherited our dad's charisma but blazed his own remarkable trail on sheer will and intellect; Don Holloway, our family patriarch, and Mary Elizabeth McConico Davis who adopted me in April of 2011 when life left me orphaned.

I'd also like to thank Alice Lewis, my Hadley Junior High School English teacher who was the first person to tell me that I could write; David Reeves, my Hadley Civics teacher who took me to Washington, D.C. for the first time; Gaye Coburn and Tommie Williams at North High School, who respectively nurtured my love for journalism and found me the scholarship money to attend college; "Daddy Sam" Adams and "Mama" Susanne Shaw at the University of Kansas (KU) School of Journalism for their loving guidance; Wichita activist Shukura Sentwali, who introduced me to Pan African thought and theory; my *Louisville Courier-Journal* family who looked out for me at work and remembered me on holidays in my first permanent job away from home, including M. David Goodwin, Larry Muhammad, Veda Morgan, Fran Jefferies, Cynthia Wilson, Fletcher and Penny Clarke and Sam Upshaw; the Rev. Dr. Kevin W. Cosby at St. Stephen Baptist Church who helped me merge my spiritual and cultural selves and stopped to pray over me at the hospital on his way to defend his doctoral dissertation; my *Wichita Eagle* family including Joe Rodriguez whose humor made work days fun and short and Dion Lefler whose stories of Pasadena made work days fun and long (smile); Tom Koetting who helped me find a writing voice and Marcia Werts and Kevin McGrath who picked up where Koetting left off; Tom Shine who taught me the importance of humor and composure as a manager, then-Managing Editor Janet Coats who hired me away from the *Courier-Journal* and gave me opportunities to grow professionally, then-Editor Rick Thames for promoting me into management and eventually to columnist; special thanks to Van E. Williams, my inspiration as a dad and someone who epitomizes "ride or die" friendship, hard work and devotion to family.

I'd like to also offer special thanks to the Honorable Gwynne Birzer, one of the most consequential people in my life; Carlota Ponds, Ed O'Malley, Matt Jordan and Shaun Rojas, Sue Dondlinger and Keshia Ezerendu from the Kansas Leadership Center; Charles F. McAfee and his unmatched knowledge of local and national African American history and his amazing ties to seemingly anyone of consequence.

A special thanks also to William and Shirley Sanders for their loving example of faith, family and fun, and to their son Barry, one of the most generous and remarkable people I'll ever meet and someone I'm lucky to call friend.

A Note on the Title

The title, "Some Were Paupers, Some Were Kings" emerged from Hank Williams' 1951 Country and Western standard, "Men With Broken Hearts."

My father recited those lines to me once as we passed homeless men sleeping on a downtown Los Angeles sidewalk when I was a child: "Some were paupers, some were kings, some were masters of their arts, but in all their shame, they were all the same, those men with broken hearts."

Blue Cedar Press editors saw parallels in those lyrics and in my columns—an attempt to strike a universal chord with each new reporting and writing foray.

You'll have to decide if I achieved such a noble objective, but that was certainly my ambition.

Contents

FOREWORD BY ED O'MALLEY, PRESIDENT AND CEO, KANSAS LEADERSHIP CENTER

I moved to Wichita almost 11 years ago and did what any son of a former journalist would do—I subscribed to the local newspaper, out of a sense of civic duty and to get up to speed on the local issues. Mark McCormick's columns in *The Wichita Eagle* quickly became one of my favorite parts of the paper for three reasons.

First, Mark's columns almost always taught me something. There was new information, a new perspective that I hadn't thought about or a lesson that I needed to learn. Sometimes I didn't want to learn the lesson, but the columns got through to me anyway.

Second, the columns were provocative. Mark wasn't afraid to raise the heat on his readers. But unlike so many columnists and opinion writers today, Mark wasn't throwing bombs or propagating fake news or half-truths. Mark was trying to get his readers to consider new truths, but he was also quite transparent with his readers and I was often left feeling Mark was always opening himself to new truths too. As he learned and explored more about community and civic issues, his views would evolve. Through his columns, he modeled what it looks like to explore tough interpretations.

And third, Mark's columns were just great writing. From word choice to sentence structure, Mark writes as I wish I could.

I had a chance to meet Mark a year after I arrived in Wichita. We were speaking on a panel together. I felt as giddy as if I were meeting another one of my favorite columnists, David Brooks or Peggy Noonan. We agreed to meet for breakfast a few weeks after the panel discussion and professional and personal relationships were born.

I've come to understand Mark as a master story teller. That's really what he does. Each column told a story, but the collection of columns tells a broader story too. Every speech I've heard Mark deliver is full of stories. As the Executive Director of the Kansas African American Museum, Mark and his team promote and tell stories so critical for the future of Kansas.

Like the best story tellers, Mark makes you think and keeps you thinking. The stories roll over and over in your head, as you wrestle with how you or your thinking is reflected in the story. Sometimes I was left feeling proud, other times conflicted and still other times indicted. But I always felt Mark's stories had a higher purpose. He wasn't just entertaining me. He wasn't just throwing together a column to collect a paycheck. His columns were stories meant to inspire action. They were his vehicle to help move our community forward.

More than just a just a collection of columns, this book is meant to inspire and inform anyone trying to make a difference in their community. I'm certain Mark hopes that any inspiration and information you find in his writing will prompt you to advance the common good of your community.

That seemed to be his intent every time he sat down in front of his keyboard.

I. BLACK COFFEE

"If I have a cup of coffee that is too strong for me because it is too black, I weaken it by pouring cream into it. I integrate it with cream. If I keep pouring enough cream in the coffee, pretty soon the entire flavor of the coffee is changed; the very nature of the coffee is changed. If enough cream is poured in, eventually you don't even know that I had coffee in this cup."

Malcolm X, "Message to the Grassroots," November 10, 1963

SECRET ADMIRER MAY WEAR WHITE SHEET*

April 16, 2003

So many people find themselves staring out from heart-break's promontory, wondering if true love ever will find them. But I'm one of the lucky ones. I have a secret admirer. Every so often, she leaves me voice mail so overflowing with passion that it would be unsuitable for me to share in this column.

I often wonder about her: Her hair. Her face. Her dreams. Sometimes, I even imagine what she's wearing. From the content of her messages, I'd guess a flowing white sheet and a matching pointed dunce hat. During the past year, she's given me several pet names. Her favorite is the N-word. I'm also her sweet "Affirmative Action Tar Baby."

She's as dependable as she is attentive. Whenever I write, she quickly responds. And as thoughtful as you please. She's careful never to call while I'm at work, presumably because she doesn't want to disturb me.

But honestly, she does sound a little disturbed. I wrote a column recently about how black families should not have to shoulder the responsibility of integration alone. She called to share in her own special way. She said white parents don't want their children going to school with "Tashanika and DeQuan-Jamall"—I'm guessing here; her words weren't clear—"or whatever ridiculous names you people give your kids. . . . My kids are in private school."

Honeysuckle called back to say, "When they don't have names like that, they have names like Jonathan and Reggie"—a reference to the Carr brothers, the two young black men who robbed five young people one night and killed four of them.

She called again after a column about how our inner demons of bigotry could prove as toxic as our external terrorist foes. I got this voice mail soon after: "Well you're

They operate without names and without return phone numbers, firing fearful missives from anonymity's grassy knoll.

wrong again, dumbs-t."

Too many Americans still don't believe people like this exist. But they do. We rarely encourage them by writing about them, because they don't represent the vast majority of Americans. But such bigots do exist, and they don't live in caves. They live downtown and in suburbs, in wealthy enclaves and in hopeless poverty. They have children in public schools and, as Dumplin' says, in private schools. They operate without names and without return phone numbers, firing fearful missives from anonymity's grassy knoll.

These connections are the unfriendly fire that journalists encounter in our efforts to connect with readers. We place e-mail addresses and desk phone numbers at the end of most of our stories because we're reaching out, trying to connect. But when casting in public waters for those connections, we sometimes hook people like my Honeybunch. After 15 years of writing professionally, comments such as hers just don't sting anymore.

Frankly, I really hope love does find her. It would be a shame to waste all that passion.

'Anything But Black,'

In an Effort to Reach All Minorities, the Unique Story of Black People Is Being Diluted

September 28, 1996

It's rare to hear as many different definitions of one term as were posited during a recent discussion of multiculturalism at Wichita State University. To some, it was as simple as Rodney King's pained exclamation, "Can't we all get along?" To others, it boiled down to respecting ethnic identity. To still others, it represented an attack on the mainstream culture.

The concerns of a white woman about succeeding in the workplace are not the same as the concerns of a black man.

But having visited several of the Diversity Week events on the campus and having spent some time with students, a new definition of multiculturalism is quickly emerging in my mind. That definition is: Anything but black. Increasingly, it seems that under the banner of multiculturalism, black people are finding their experiences mixed in with the experiences of other groups of people. And that makes me uneasy.

There is a real tension between the idea that black people do not want to be singled out for different treatment, and the idea that black people need to be singled out because their experience is so different from any other group in this country's history. My fear is that by embracing vague notions of "multiculturalism" or "diversity," people might be able to avoid dealing with uniquely African American issues. And in the process, the social justice issues of black folks will be watered down, glossed over or completely ignored.

Ethnic and cultural identity is important, but comparing the historical and social plight of black people to that of recent and often affluent immigrants, and calling the whole movement multiculturalism, dilutes and trivializes the African American push for social justice. At the university, I heard a lot of people calling for more tolerance of people's clothes or their music or their religion, all of which are worthwhile sentiments.

But the black experience in this country goes so much deeper than that. The attempts of a Malaysian student to feel comfortable at WSU are not the same as the attempts of a black student who grew up a block away from campus. The concerns of a white woman about succeeding in the workplace are not the same as the concerns of a black man. The story of Middle Eastern immigrants is not interchangeable with the story of African American slaves.

Sure, I am oversimplifying a bit to make the point. But black students at WSU told me this week that while they were participating in Diversity Week activities, they felt pushed into the margins. "It's more for international students," said Rhianna Gentry, a St. Louis sophomore who is black. "They (organizers of Diversity Week) are catering to people from India, Malaysia, Iraq and so on." Kia Everett, a Kansas City sophomore who is black, said she and some other students feel a little jilted, although there was no tension between the groups.

Black students simply will have to continue doing what they've always done on majority white campuses—creating their own community for themselves, and doing their own thing. But in the process, it occurs to me, black people have gone from carrying other groups on their coattails to being left out in the cold without a coat—at least without a coat they can call their own.

And this idea of anything but black goes far beyond just one campus or one week of activities. After a generation of having only a few hours of soul music on a local radio station—it was called "Soul Sunday"—Wichita eventually got an urban contemporary radio station. But these days, thanks to what I see as the anything but black principle, soulful Luther Vandross gives way to crossover artists Ace of Base, and suddenly an urban contemporary station becomes just another top-40 outlet.

Studies have shown that the spoils of hard-won civil

rights battles have most often benefited white women who have been granted limited or honorary minority status. And there have been numerous organizations and programs in Wichita, in Kansas and across the nation that did good work for black people and the black community, but had their funding threatened unless they took their focus off "blacks" and replaced them with "minorities." Many universities used to have a black studies department and now, many of them have minority studies departments.

My favorite sentiment from Malcolm X comes to mind. Malcolm X said that coffee does its job best—keeping you awake and alert—when it's hot and black and strong. But when you start adding milk and cream and sugar, it's no longer hot, it's no longer black and it's no longer strong enough to keep you awake. Some people might prefer the taste of that kind of coffee; maybe it goes down a little easier and doesn't have too much of a jolt.

I like my coffee black.

ONE NATION, INDIVISIBLE: WHAT WILL IT TAKE?*

November 12, 2008

We were asking each other, 'What have we done to them to make them hate us so much?'

So who are we really? Is America the country where a poor, black child raised by white grandparents can become President, or the country where Alice Love's granddaughter tells her she lost her playmate because of the election's outcome?

Are we the country where the most diverse demographic coalition ever assembled elected its candidate? Or the country where Alice's daughter dreads going back to work this week at a local fast-food restaurant because a few patrons have sunken to calling employees the N-word and saying they couldn't wait for the assassination of President-elect Barack Obama?

"A lot of people are having a hard time with this," Love called to tell me Monday.

This moment may represent the nation's best opportunity to pivot out of a painful past. But disturbing images have surfaced since the US elected its first black president.

These folks don't represent most of us. They're just a comparatively few frustrated folks making our transition to a more conciliatory era tougher. A colleague of mine said her 22-year-old nephew in North Carolina needed seven stitches after a woman punched him in the eye for telling her, like it or not, Obama was her president. Racist calls to *The Eagle's* Opinion Line have spiked since the election, said Opinion Editor Phillip Brownlee.

With the jubilation last week in Chicago, in Los Angeles and in Harlem, an equal and opposite reaction elsewhere seemed certain. I soon started hearing from friends about how for the weeks before the election, they held spirited debates with co-workers about the upcoming election. But the morning after the election, nothing. No debates. No conversations. Not even eye contact in some instances.

8

Love said two other relatives and a friend have complained of problems at work. The friend, a teacher, said people she'd eaten lunch with for years have stopped talking to her. The relatives said they'd had mild dust-ups with co-workers about the election.

And then there's her daughter's experience. The young woman said a small number of customers Monday, in response to some small aggravation over their order, called her and other employees the N-word and told them not to touch their food or money. "We were asking each other, 'What have we done to them to make them hate us so much?' " said the young woman, who didn't want her first name used because one of the hostile patrons is a regular customer. The manager, she said, asked them to blow it off and not worry about it.

On the surface, these vignettes boil down to it being easier to be a good winner than a good loser, says Ron Matson, chairman of Wichita State University's sociology department. But on a deeper level, we're seeing a reaction to a shake-up of some bedrock status assumptions, he said. "If you push someone to change who thinks they're in power because of the color of their skin, because of their position or because of their gender, you get a backlash," Matson said. "That kind of shaking can be disconcerting."

If tough times don't create character but reveal it, what's our character? Are we a place where little girls can't play together after a black man wins the presidency? Are we the one nation, indivisible, as we claim to be? Not until this behavior, a fixture of a tragic past, resides there permanently.

WHEN COLLEAGUES COUNT YOU OUT

October 11, 1997

It wasn't simply a matter of journalists not being able to count. They can count when they want to.

I saw a buddy of mine awhile back. I like talking to him. We always seem to be on the same wavelength. This day was no different. He was smiling that tight-lipped smile of his and he asked me what I thought about the Promise Keepers gathering in Washington, then still a couple of days away.

"I'm just waiting to see how they count it," I said, and we both burst out laughing. We knew exactly what was going to happen. A full national mall that weekend was going to equal a million people, or at least more people than had gathered there for 1995's Million Man March.

And sure enough, flipping from newscast to newscast last Saturday evening, four commentators put the number of Promise Keepers on the mall at "about a million." A fifth said "well over a million." *The Eagle* implied that there were more people at the Promise Keepers rally, but didn't base it on any objective criteria. It just "appeared" larger, the article said.

I covered the Million Man March two years ago, making the trip with a group of Wichita men and recording their experiences. I can remember first the shock, and then the hurt on everyone's face the day after the march when the "official" count estimated the crowd at only 400,000, the figure quoted in a wire story *The Eagle* ran on the front page the day after.

A later, independent count put the number somewhere between 800,000 and 1.2 million, but by then that was a little like trying to put the manure back into the bull. Messy. The men I'd traveled with tried to remind each other that it didn't matter what anyone else thought. They made the trip for themselves and for their families, not the media. But many lamented privately that the low count hurt them.

It trivialized what they thought was a noble, historic accomplishment.

It wasn't simply a matter of journalists not being able to count. They can count when they want to. It is more a reminder that, sometimes, minorities don't count. That message comes through clearly—albeit subtly—to black journalists each time we get wind of co-workers talking about how the company is hiring too many minorities or that there are too many black faces on the front page.

I'm not attacking the Promise Keepers march. As a Christian, I was moved by the event. My favorite moment each Sunday is the moment at the end of the sermon when "the doors of the church are opened," and people walk down the aisle and give their lives to Jesus. On a great day, eight or ten people make that walk. In contrast, the sight of all those people on the mall—a million or not—recommitting themselves to Christ was absolutely humbling.

I'm not trying to say that the Promise Keepers are the darlings of the media. I wish I had a dime for every example of anti-Christian bias I saw in the reporting. Journalists continually pointing out how racially diverse the crowd was, for example—when racial reconciliation was one of the founding planks of the organization—was just another example of how uncomfortable the mainstream media are with the issue of religion and how we don't get it sometimes.

That said, I want to leave my colleagues with a bit of American history that they're seemingly unclear on.

Turn with me in your US history textbooks to the issue of proportional representation. Proportional representation, as we have in the US House of Representatives, necessitated a means of counting population, which meant that the delegates assembling our government had to come to terms with the issue of slavery.

Southern states wanted slaves counted among their populations; northern states wanted to exclude slaves from population tallies. Their solution, the "Three-Fifths Compromise," stated that each black person would be counted as three-fifths of a human being.

Journalists must have been using some form of this formula when they counted only 400,000 black men on the mall in 1995, and so many more men on the mall last weekend. Clearly, they're unaware that the compromise is no longer in effect.

SAVOR THE PRESENT

February 1, 2006

The fact that I realized a lifelong dream of owning a home last year shouldn't crack a chapter in any history book.

A knowledgeable real estate agent and helpful mortgage lender made buying a house just about headache free. I never once felt anyone steering me away from any neighborhood. The only attention my closing brought from neighbors consisted of welcoming plates of cookies and pleasant waves.

But 42 years earlier, less than a mile from my home, the purchase of a house by a black family inflamed neighbors. It's one of those stories, particularly as I ponder the death of civil rights icon Coretta Scott King, that makes Black History Month such a personally important time.

When famed civil rights lawyer Chester Lewis and his wife, Vashti, decided to buy a home, they settled on an affluent neighborhood north of Wichita State University. They knew the area, between Hillside and Oliver north of 21st Street, as a white neighborhood, and they suspected real estate agents wouldn't sell or even show them a home there. So they asked a white couple to arrange the visits and had Vashti tag along as the couple's live-in maid. When Vashti decided on a house, the white couple went to the closing and deeded the property to the Lewises.

An account of the maneuver appears in the book *Dissent in Wichita* by Friends University Professor Gretchen Eick. "From the time they moved into their new home, the Lewises were pressured to leave," the book says. "A neighbor, Charles Fisher, chaired a group of 60 to 80 people from the neighborhood united in their determination to keep African Americans out of the area . . . 'Of course, we would like to see Lewis leave,' *The Eagle* quoted Fisher as saying in July 1963."

Someone set off explosives in the Lewises' mailbox.

Volunteers from Temple Emanu-El and the Unitarian Church formed nightly watch teams to protect the family.

Someone threw a brick through their window. Someone poured kerosene on the front yard in the shape of a cross and set it ablaze. Someone killed the family cat. Volunteers from Temple Emanu-El and the Unitarian Church formed nightly watch teams to protect the family.

Other black families that moved into the area shared similar stories of fear and intimidation, Eick said, adding that real estate agents made a lot of money peddling fear. Real estate agents, she said, often placed fliers in mailboxes warning white homeowners that their property values would nose-dive because a black family had bought a house in the neighborhood.

Whatever wounds homeowners incurred though, were self-inflicted, she said. Multiple homes up for sale at the same time on the same street killed prices, not a new black homeowner next door. "It shows the nastiness of the racism and how housing tended to be the hardest area to transform, to open up," she said.

Even now, a legislative bill seeks to force some home associations with restrictive covenants banning minorities from owning or renting property to strike racist language.

Thanks to Mr. Lewis, Mrs. King, and others, I didn't have to worry about any of that when I bought a home. The Lewises paid those closing costs through worried days and sleepless nights, and a dream for something better for the people who followed them.

I think of them every night as I'm closing my garage door, especially during February. I think about how so much of what I have—dreams, opportunities, rights—I didn't actually have to pay for.

Getting the Job, Getting the Job Done

March 16, 2006

There was a time in our country when an African American getting an appointment meant more than someone merely getting a job. I've celebrated such events. I wrote a year or so ago about the changing face of Wichita leadership. A black city manager. A black vice mayor. A black police chief.

We—society, black and white—often equate the attainment of a job or position by someone from a minority class with progress. Racial advancement. The first black this and the first black that. Then we say, "Haven't we come a long way?" Maybe not. Front-burner racial issues have moved from black and white to multiculturalism and now, in many cases, black on black. It's a sign of the complexities that accompany complexion.

A group of Wichita police officers filed a discrimination lawsuit Wednesday against their police chief who, like them, is black. An astonishing and fascinating turn of events.

Didn't Norman Williams, this black chief, work his way through the ranks to become chief? Didn't he only recently promote a black woman? If he could invest his talents and intellect in this system and eventually become chief, then surely the system, though imperfect, works—right? A man who fought his way through discrimination wouldn't tolerate it once he was in authority, would he?

The named plaintiffs in the class-action suit claim he has. Through their lawyer, Uzo Ohaebosim, the officers claim Williams tolerates intolerance among supervisors working directly under him. "The chief is actively fostering an environment that promotes discrimination," Ohaebosim said.

When Williams was named chief in 2000, some of these

It is worth noting that in this litigious society, the officers aren't asking for monetary damages, only systemic policy changes.

officers left the Fraternal Order of Police, which they said opposed his appointment. They said they expected fairness, not favoritism, as a result of the appointment. But instead of fairness, the officers said they were treated more harshly, presumably because Williams didn't want to appear to favor black officers.

Ohaebosim said the officers met with Williams at least four times to discuss the issues but reached only an impasse. "He can't say that he doesn't know," Ohaebosim said. Police spokeswoman Janet Johnson said the department didn't see the lawsuit coming. "We haven't seen it," she said of the filing when I called for comment. "We can't comment on something we're not even aware of." Williams did not return a call.

Lawsuits can so often amount to finger-pointing. The courts will sort all of this out. It is worth noting that in this litigious society, the officers aren't asking for monetary damages, only systemic policy changes. "There is a problem," Ohaebosim said, "and it has not been addressed."

Maybe part of the lesson here is to be cautious about equating a single appointment with the advancement of an entire race. Institutions, regardless of who runs them, can prove complex organisms resistant to change. What an awful burden it must be to carry the hopes and aspirations of individuals and institutions into an office with you. I can't imagine what it must be like to be Chief Williams.

But if anyone were equipped to deal with this situation, it's him, a man who stands astride two cultures, two realities. There's room to improve the department, whether or not these allegations are true. And when he does, we can cheer not simply because he got the job, but because he got the job done.

ARE THESE GUYS FELONS
BECAUSE THEY'RE WHITE?

September 16, 2005

Scenes of looters sloshing through New Orleans' devastated streets led to the typical anthropological study of black culture in general. Pundits pondered what prompted the pillaging. Poverty? Racism? Disintegration of families?

I have a new set of questions, based on the corporate plundering of Topeka-based Westar Energy by two of its executives. Questions you won't hear on the evening news or in news accounts. Questions you won't hear from talking heads because these looters are white.

A federal jury found former Westar execs David Wittig and Doug Lake guilty Monday of "looting the utility" of millions of dollars, according to a story in *The Eagle*. The government has asked Wittig to repay $27.9 million and Lake to repay $9.4 million.

A jury ordered the pair to hand over millions of dollars in cash on Thursday, but far less than federal prosecutors had sought. The same jury had found that the two conspired to steal money from Westar, sidestepped accounting controls, and committed wire fraud and money laundering. Among other things, Wittig spent $6 million of Westar money renovating his Topeka home, a mansion formerly owned by Kansas Governor Alf Landon.

And let's be clear here. They actually looted the utility. They didn't just find this money. So here are my questions, again, questions you won't hear about this crime: Is this a cultural trait, something rooted perhaps in the DNA or at least the historical behavior of white CEOs? Aren't most corporate looters white—as in the cases of the people who led WorldCom, Enron, Arthur Andersen and Adelphia Communications? Isn't the single best indicator of white-collar crime in an area the percentage of white male CEOs?

A few more questions: Was it Wittig and Lake's upbringing or some tragic breakdown of the white nuclear family that drove them to steal? Maybe if their parents had done a better job of child rearing, these brats wouldn't have grown up to mug decent, hardworking folks. And speaking of family, shouldn't we be concerned about their children looting? Could corporate raiders be passing this proclivity down from generation to generation?

Shouldn't we talk to some white ministers or sociologists about the coldness and ruthlessness embedded in white-run boardrooms? A coldness that allows executives to accept bonuses larger than the salaries of people they're laying off?

What implications will this drumbeat of corporate scandals have for white society? Why doesn't someone in white America stand up and denounce this behavior and stop playing the 'corporate card' and accusing us of being anti-business when we simply want an accounting?

Aren't these the same folks constantly preaching to us about personal responsibility as a conservative trait? Or do they actually worship at the altars of NASDAQ and the New York Stock Exchange? Maybe you won't hear these questions because we didn't actually see looped, televised images of Wittig and Lake wading through the lives they'd ruined, carrying the millions of dollars they stole while holding up sagging britches. They did their dirty work in a board room, wielding sharp pencils and wearing fine suits and silk ties. I'm not excusing what the displaced looters did. But if the theft of guns and televisions and liquor by black men provokes a broad sociological inventory about black culture, why doesn't the looting of millions of dollars from corporations by white men warrant a similar inventory of white culture?

I say it does. The question is, though, will it ever actually happen?

[These convictions were later overturned on appeal.]

THIS "EPIDEMIC" SHOULD NOT COME AS A SURPRISE

October 8, 1995

The reaction to last Tuesday's verdict in the O.J. Simpson double murder trial reminded me of one of comedian Richard Pryor's most powerful routines. Pryor would immerse himself in a character fighting drug addiction. He would slur his words, stumble across the stage and talk to imaginary people around him. "Slow that car down, fool, this is a neighborhood, not a residential district," he would yell.

The audience would roar with laughter. But Pryor's character eventually would find a fix, and while he was winding the rubber tubing around his arm and then pulling it tightly with his teeth, the laughter would start to die. By the time he slapped the fleshy side of his forearm, trying to find a vein, the laughter was almost gone. And by the time he squeezed the poison into his vein, there was silence.

Pryor, still in character, would collapse. But he wasn't done yet. After a moment, he would bounce back up and start talking about how people like his addicted character dot countless comers of the nation's inner cities, and how an endless stream of people pass by at a safe distance and comment on how sad it is to see a human being in such condition. But when those same people find out their 14-year-old son or daughter is high on cocaine, they scream: "Oh my God, it's an epidemic! Something must be done!"

"Maybe next time," Pryor would say in closing, "when you see a black man in trouble, you'll stop and help." The last sentence was a sledgehammer. In the audience, there seemed a clear division between those who were enthusiastically supportive and those who were bitterly disappointed by the message. Sort of like Tuesday.

For the last few days, our newspapers and television screens have been filled with people who were enthusiastically supportive and those who were bitterly disappointed by the Simpson verdict. In the process, the verdict has highlighted the fundamental differences in the way black people and white people view the world.

Where black people saw former Simpson friend Ronald Shipp as an Uncle Tom, white people saw him as a consistent, credible witness. Where black people saw defense attorney Johnnie Cochran as a heroic defender of rights, white people saw him as a race-baiter. Where black people saw a case full of holes, white people saw insurmountable evidence.

Make no mistake I'm not trying to diminish the horror of what happened to Brown and Goldman. I know what it is like to lose someone who is close.

And along the way, I've noticed those white people talking about dismantling the justice system. They say justice has not been served, that something is terribly wrong with the system, that something needs to be done to make the system fairer. This newspaper even printed an editorial cartoon of Lady Justice on her knees, reaching for the door of a battered women's shelter.

In other words, the one time in a high profile case that the system works for a black person, white people say it needs to be uprooted. Just like Pryor's routine, this is "Oh my God, it's an epidemic" all over again.

Where were all these people in years past? Where were they when all-white juries set white killers of black people free time and time again? Where were they when Emmett Till was killed? Or Medgar Evers? Where were they when the phrase, "It's not the justice system, it's the just-us system," became a cliché in the black community because the system so often seemed for whites only?

And where are they today? In Philadelphia, 60 convictions have been overturned after an investigation uncovered deep corruption within the police department. Officers have pleaded guilty to faking evidence and framing people. Hundreds more cases could be reviewed; the scandal is worsening almost daily. And most of the victims are black.

But there is no one on *Larry King Live* calling for a revamping of the justice system because of the Philadelphia system. No, it took the deaths of Nicole Brown Simpson and Ron Goldman to spark that kind of sentiment. Make no mistake I'm not trying to diminish the horror of what happened to Brown and Goldman. I know what it is like to lose someone who is close.

But the reaction to the case involving them has pointed out again that sadly, black people and white people in this country don't really know each other. We grow up with different experiences and perspectives. We're friendly, but not often friends. We rarely live together. We rarely go to church together. We only work together, and even those relationships are often strained or superficial.

How else could we be looking at the same thing and come away seeing things so differently? How else could some of us be so surprised at an epidemic that the rest of us have been living with for generations?

Recalling Hollowell's Greatness

January 2, 2005

He regularly risked his life representing penniless black defendants in front of all white juries in the darkest reaches of the segregated South. . .

In the midst of President Bill Clinton's lurid affair with Monica Lewinsky and talk of impeachment, Washington lawyer and presidential confidant Vernon Jordan was perhaps the most sought-after interview in the country. Jordan, after all, was reportedly the man who helped arrange a job for Lewinsky after her White House internship.

Jordan granted precious few interview requests during that span. One of them was mine. I wasn't calling in search of sordid details of the president's Oval Office tryst. Rather, I wanted to know what impact a daring lawyer named Donald Hollowell—a Wichita native adopted by Atlanta as "Mr. Civil Rights"—had had on his life. "He gave me my first job," said Jordan, who once worked as Mr. Hollowell's law clerk. "He saw that I had something in me and he found it, tapped it, nurtured it. He has touched many young people. I personally owe him a great debt of gratitude."

It impressed me that a man of Jordan's stature would call at the mere mention of Mr. Hollowell's name. Even more amazing, though, was that so few people knew of his courageous career. Mr. Hollowell died of heart failure last week at 87, but he leaves behind a towering civil rights career everyone should know about.

Probably Mr. Hollowell's most famous client was the Rev. Martin Luther King Jr., whom he helped free from Reidsville Prison in 1960 with the help of Dodgers great Jackie Robinson, crooner Frank Sinatra and Sinatra's friend, John F. Kennedy, who happened to be running for president at the time.

But in my conversations with him, Mr. Hollowell seemed most proud of the work he did alone. He regularly risked his life representing penniless black defendants in

22

front of all white juries in the darkest reaches of the seg-regated South. And he fought for them as though he were fighting for King.

Mr. Hollowell was a larger-than-life figure who entered this world December 19, 1917, on Indiana Street. He at-tended L'Ouverture Elementary and later moved with his family to Augusta, Eureka and Leavenworth. He joined the famed Buffalo Soldiers at Fort Leavenworth as a high school junior before leaving Kansas to make his mark on the American South, traveling a gravel-road gauntlet of

Don Hollowell. Courtesy The Wichita Eagle/Travis Haying.

county sheriffs to help black defendants.

Some of those courtrooms seemed hostile even by that era's standards. Jordan recalled in our phone interview, "There was one judge, a W.I. Geer, who was known as, W. 'I.-don't-want-any-niggers-in-my-court' Geer in Blakely, Georgia," Jordan said. But Mr. Hollowell freed people— including a 15-year-old boy sentenced to death—despite the way such judges denied his motions, overruled his ob-jections, and kept their thumbs on justice's scale.

. . . And he fought for them as though he were fighting for King.

He'd later win the case that integrated the University of Georgia as well as others that added black doctors and dentists to hospital staffs. His legal reputation spread across the South and touched people like Jordan. "It was instructive, inspiring, and consistent with what I went to law school to do," Jordan recalled. "I was lucky to be associated with someone of his character and fearlessness."

Thinking back, I shouldn't have been so surprised that Jordan made himself available for that interview. He wasn't about to let an opportunity to talk about Mr. Hollowell pass. And neither will I.

A GIANT WON MAJOR BATTLES, BUT NOT FAME

July 20, 2005

I consider myself fairly informed. Yet every once in a while, I run across someone I've never heard of whose achievements soar higher than mountains. Someone whose contribution carries such weight and depth and breadth that I ask myself, how could I not know about this person?

Former Kansan Arthur Fletcher sits atop that list. He died of a heart attack last week in his Washington, D.C. home. He was 80. Fletcher, who graduated from Junction City High School and earned a degree at Washburn University, served as vice president of the Kansas Republican Party in the 1950s, ran for president in 1996, and advised four US presidents. He was assistant secretary of labor in the Nixon administration, deputy assistant for urban affairs in the Ford administration, an adviser in the Reagan administration, and chairman of the Civil Rights Commission during the first Bush administration.

His party, he said, was abandoning minorities and the working class in favor of the rich and affluent.

He fought under Gen. George C. Patton in World War II and earned a Purple Heart. He was a 6-foot-4 defensive end for the Los Angeles Rams and was the Baltimore Colts' first black player. He earned his law degree in 1950 from Chicago's LaSalle Extension University.

He coined the phrase "A mind is a terrible thing to waste" as executive director for the United Negro College Fund.

He's also called the father of affirmative action. As assistant labor secretary in the late 1960s, he devised a plan requiring Philadelphia federal construction companies to set goals for hiring minorities and to make good-faith efforts to meet the goals on hiring minorities or face sanctions. The plan, often derided for its reliance on counting and numbers, became the affirmative action model. "We have no problem counting who's on welfare, we have no problem counting who's in jail, we have no problem counting who's on AFDC," he once told *The Eagle.* "What's wrong with counting success?"

Yet for all of his success, there were many things he couldn't do. He told *The Eagle* in a 1995 interview that he couldn't play college football in Kansas in the 1940s because three of the Big Six schools wouldn't play a team with a black player. He said he couldn't teach in Kansas public schools because it meant instructing white girls. He attended Washburn under the G.I. Bill but couldn't live in on-campus G.I. housing. He graduated and played professional football, but no white employers would hire him. So he got a job delivering ice. "I'm a college graduate iceman and the joke of the town," Fletcher told *The Eagle.*

Arthur Fletcher,
Department of Labor photo

Famed former Kansas governor Alf Landon later helped him launch a political career as a Republican. Still, he said, he couldn't keep his party from abandoning historic roots planted by Lincoln, according to an expansive obituary in *The Washington Post.*

While serving as an adviser to President Ronald Reagan, he called Reagan "the worst president for civil rights in this century." And while chairman of the Civil Rights Commission, he pounded President George H. W. Bush for labeling civil rights legislation a quota bill. His party, he said, was abandoning minorities and the working class in favor of the rich and affluent.

All of these honorable battles, and I didn't know him. I think I know why, and maybe the reason isn't so bad. He so successfully built a new world that many people, including me, never had to see the old one.

Thank you, Mr. Fletcher, for my blissful ignorance.

Follow Civil Rights Martyr's Lead on November 2

October 13, 2004

The Rev. James Reeb could have stayed home. The Unitarian Universalist minister and Wichita native worked with poor people in his new home of Boston. Like work at preventing crime and hunger, work with the poor can trail on endlessly.

But Reeb answered the Rev. Martin Luther King, Jr.' s call in March 1965 to come to Selma, Alabama, to participate in a voting rights march to Montgomery. Lucky for all of us who intend to vote November 2 that he did.

Reeb, born here in 1927, traveled to the fault line of the struggle for black voting rights two days after state troopers had brutally beaten back marchers in what came to be known as "Bloody Sunday." Only two weeks earlier at another voting rights demonstration, a law enforcement officer had shot and killed Jimmie Lee Jackson, a black hospital worker and Vietnam veteran, as Jackson tried to protect his mother from being beaten. There had been other incidents before and in between.

King had called for ministers nationwide to descend on Selma, vowing that the protest march would move forward. He'd organized a planning meeting one evening for shortly after the dinner hour.

Reeb and two other men decided to dine in a black part of town before the meeting. The following account comes from the Rev. Clark Olsen, who accompanied Reeb and the Rev. Orloff Miller that night: After eating, the trio headed back to the church on a shorter route which, unknown to them, passed through a tough white neighborhood. Suddenly, they noticed some men watching them from across the street. One carried a club.

"I do remember Orloff and Jim saying, 'Just keep walking,' " Olsen said in an April 2000 interview in *The*

"It's part of the story of civil rights, and the tragedy of civil rights, that it was the death of a white minister that was the final impetus to the passage of the Voting Rights Act," Olsen said in the interview. . .

New York Times. Civil rights volunteers, he said, were taught not to resist if attacked, but to fall to the ground, covering their heads. The men came up behind the ministers and Olsen looked back just as one man swung a club at Reeb, striking his head. The sound, Olsen said, was "just awful."

Reeb collapsed, Miller dropped to the sidewalk, covering his head. Olsen tried to run; but was caught and punched, his glasses sent flying. The attackers fled. A frightening night ensued as Olsen and Miller, each with minor injuries, tried to get help for Reeb. He died two days later.

". . .The deaths of any number of blacks had not received anywhere the amount of attention."

President Lyndon B. Johnson called the events in Selma "an American tragedy" that should strengthen people's determination "to bring full and equal and exact justice to all of our people." Johnson's voting rights proposal had reached Congress the Monday after Reeb's death and Johnson's signing of the act prohibited the denial or abridgment of the right to vote based on race.

"It's part of the story of civil rights, and the tragedy of civil rights, that it was the death of a white minister that was the final impetus to the passage of the Voting Rights Act," Olsen said in the interview. "The deaths of any number of blacks had not received anywhere the amount of attention."

I saw a photograph of Reeb hanging in the National Civil Rights Museum in Memphis last August, and I understand that people have erected a memorial to him and others who died for the cause of voting rights in Selma. As far as I know, Reeb may be Wichita's only civil rights martyr. But his legacy is less about how bravely he died than about how boldly he lived. When it would have been easier and certainly safer to stay home, Reeb didn't.

And as the voting registration deadline and Election Day near, neither should you.

A MONUMENT TO DIGNITY IN ADVERSITY

May 30, 2004

The memorial Bessie Halbrook and six other women established nearly 60 years ago stands on the southern edge of McAdams Park, virtually forgotten. Two sentinel sycamores shade the monument, Wichita's first World War II memorial, in the parking lot in front of the park's baseball stadium.

Its inscription reads simply: "In honor of the men and women who served in the armed forces of the USA during the second World War, erected by the "Double V Victorettes." "We were just a group of ladies who wanted to do something," said Halbrook, now 96.

That's hardly the whole story. The story begins and ends in Wichita but touched soldiers around the world with the help of black newspapers like *The Pittsburgh* (Pennsylvania) *Courier.* In the years leading up to World War II Robert L. Vann's *Courier* circulated nationally and offered black readers a weekly shot of racial adrenaline with columnists like W.E.B. DuBois and novelist Zora Neale Hurston.

Perhaps the paper's most significant contribution grew out of a letter from a Wichita reader. James Thompson, a cafeteria worker, wrote *The Courier* encouraging black people to support the World War II effort while pressing for change in American society. "Should I sacrifice my life to live half American?" Thompson asked in his letter. "Let us colored Americans adopt the Double V for a double victory. The first V, for victory over our enemies without. The second V, for victory over our enemies from within."

Letters of support flooded *The Courier*, which sponsored Double V events, sold Double V decals. And published front-page Double V articles.

The campaign energized a group of patriotic women here, one of them a young Bessie Halbrook. She and six

Little by little, most people forgot about the monument. They forgot the patriotism it must have taken for black women to build it in a nation that made them drink from separate water fountains.

other women—Erma Carter Younger, Mary Williams House, Myrtle Younger Mitchell, Opal House Nulan, Lola Groomer Barker and Dorothy Jones Penny—formed a group called the Victorettes. During the war, they sent care packages to soldiers. After the war, they planned a memorial for "our soldiers who came back and the ones who didn't," Halbrook said.

Between selling cookies and asking businesses and clubs for donations, they raised the $1,000 they needed. Quiring Monument Co. cut the stone and the women placed the memorial in McKinley Park—now McAdams Park. Although park officials moved the monument farther south to make way for tennis courts, it has stood in the park since 1946.

When she was able physically, Halbrook said, she and House visited it every year and put flowers there. Neither has been able to do that for a while.

Little by little, most people forgot about the monument. They forgot the patriotism it must have taken for black women to build it in a nation that made them drink from separate water fountains. They forgot that for all of its horrors, World War II held deep meaning and hope of a better life for many African Americans.

In a larger sense, the memorial ties all of us to a time of shared sacrifice, when the ripples of war touched us so much more personally, whether it was limiting our travel, tightening our belts for meatless meals or collecting reams of aluminum or piles of rubber. A simple dignity flows through that monument's history. A dignity befitting people like Halbrook. A dignity worth honoring this holiday weekend.

BROWN V. BOE EVENT UNLIKELY STAGE FOR BUSH

May 16, 2004

President Bush will attend the *Brown v. Board of Education* 50th anniversary ceremonies Monday in Topeka.

That's a little like him attending the Democratic National Convention later this summer. You'd think he'd feel out of place, considering his stated views and policies. The president has spent the past year backing efforts to roll back the Brown decision's influence. He joined the campaign to dismantle the University of Michigan's affirmative action admissions policy, an educational equity program.

Was he concerned that so many undeserving minority students have flooded colleges and universities that white students couldn't get in? "At the undergraduate level," Bush said of the University of Michigan program, "African American students and some Hispanic students and Native American students receive 20 points out of a maximum of 150, not because of any academic achievement or life experience, but solely because they are African American, Hispanic or Native American."

The US Supreme Court in a 5-4 decision last summer, however, upheld the use of affirmative action in college admissions. In hollow praise of the decision, Bush said the focus should be on "race-neutral" approaches to make campuses more welcoming for everyone.

But his own life has been anything but a neutral, bootstraps struggle to success. Lefty political commentator Michael Kinsley, in an insightful article last year, called President Bush perhaps "the most spectacular affirmative-action success story of all time."

"Until 1994, when he was 48 years old and got elected Governor of Texas, his life was almost empty of accomplishments. Yet bloodlines and connections had put him into Andover, Yale and Harvard Business School, and even

Attacking educational equity helps to maintain the status quo.

31

provided him with a fortune after years of business disappointments. Intelligence, hard work and the other qualities associated with the concept of merit had almost nothing to do with Bush's life and success up to that point. And yet seven years later he was President of the US."

That charmed life represents the inverse of *Brown*, which sought to open society's opportunities—in this case, education—to people beyond the privileged class. Attacking educational equity helps to maintain the status quo and continued preferences for people like him. The status quo also has meant a widening of the opportunity gap *Brown* sought to close.

The recently released documentary *Beyond Brown: Pursuing the Promise* points out the huge disparities and re-segregation in public education, in part through largely white gifted-and-talented programs and increased funding in affluent suburbs.

Despite his No Child Left Behind plan, there's virtually nothing about the president's record that says to me that he has a sense for any of this or for the intense struggle and the everyday courage it took for people in that era to simply file the papers. In fact, were he appointing Supreme Court justices in the early 1950s, we'd probably have nothing to celebrate Monday.

I have a difficult time imagining President Bush appointing civil rights-friendly judges as President Dwight D. Eisenhower, a Kansan and a Republican, did in appointing Earl Warren and four other judges to the high court. Or why Bush would want to attend ceremonies that celebrate ideas from which he seems so thoroughly disconnected.

ALL-BLACK TOWN INSTILLED DETERMINATION

February 20, 2004

Many of the hollow brick buildings lining each side of Main Street in Boley, Oklahoma sag from the weight of the decades layered on top of them. Time also has claimed many of its stalwart citizens and pock marked the town's two paved roads. But there's hope there, too. Hope from what it was—once the nation's largest all-black town—and what it represents simply by existing.

Because my parents were born there and my paternal grandparents lived in Boley, I visited several times a year. I spent many a day there as a child chasing rabbits with a pellet gun, trying to coax a perch onto my fishing line, wandering the wide fields of summer-warmed weeds and listening to stories about my grandfather, the town's chief of police for more than 50 years. I hadn't realized until I'd become an adult just how important that town and my time there really was.

Joseph Langston McCormick, the columnist's grandfather, stands in front of the Farmer's State Bank building in Boley, Oklahoma, that he and citizens of the town defended in 1932 against Charles "Pretty Boy" Floyd's gang of bank robbers. Courtesy Mark McCormick.

Booker T. Washington, founder of the National Negro Business League and the Tuskegee Institute in Alabama, visited the town in 1905 and proclaimed it to be "the most enterprising and in many ways the most interesting of the Negro towns in the United States."

Boley, about an hour's drive east of Oklahoma City, birthed one of the first black-owned banks with a national charter and one of the first black-owned electric companies. Boley also claimed one of the first black-owned telephone companies and more than 60 other black-owned businesses.

Founded in 1903, Boley began on 160 acres of land donated by my aunt Abigail Barnett McCormick. She inherited the land as the daughter of James Barnett, a Creek Freedman, the original owner. Nowhere else, neither in the Deep South nor in the far west, did so many African Americans come together to govern their own communities. From 1865 to 1920, they created more than 50 such towns and settlements all over Oklahoma. Some, like Boley, still exist.

The towns sprang from the Indian Territory after the Civil War when former slaves settled together for mutual protection and economic security. When the government forced American Indians to accept individual land allotments, most freedmen chose land next to other African Americans. They created cohesive, prosperous communities that eventually grew into towns. But like many rural towns, Boley suffered through difficult times. By World War II, the population had dropped from 4,000 to about 700. Many, like my parents, moved to Wichita.

Boley's downtown business district is listed in the National Register of Historic Places. It was the site of a heroic, citizen-aided gun battle in 1932 against Charles "Pretty Boy" Floyd's gang of bank robbers. It also hosts the nation's oldest African American community-based rodeo every Memorial Day weekend.

An incredible spirit—untouched by time—moves through the place and through the people. Former Kansas state Rep. Jonathan Wells, from all-black Taft, Oklahoma, says people from all-black towns generally have a different point of view. "They think they can rise like anyone else," Wells said. "They've usually seen black people in leadership roles, and they expect to be in leadership roles themselves. They don't expect to be passed over." I'm almost certain that my time in and my ties to Boley helped mold the "uppity" Negro that so infuriates the Opinion Line contributors who lob verbal grenades at me each week. They seem troubled that I have the temerity to form my own opinions, dream my own dreams and believe what I believe.

Does that mean that I don't have my share of doubts and fears? Of course not. What it does mean is that when doubts and fears begin to collect in my conscience, Boley's pocked roads and sagging buildings remind me of a far different story. A story about what determination, vision and hard work can accomplish. And that's no fable. Boley's existence is the proof.

LISTENING FOR WHISPERS OF FADING PAST

February 13, 2004

At yet another site, an entire troop of black soldiers is said to be buried.

In a field about 7 acres square, as recently as last year, heads of cattle grazed on what Norma Tolson believes to be historic grave sites. Someone, she said, toppled the tombstones and ripped up the barbed wire on the plot in her hometown of Weir in southeast Kansas. The ground there, she's learning, may cloak horrible stories unknown to most.

The land, Tolson insists, marked the sites where the families of black miners once laid loved ones to rest. After the families had been chased from the region decades ago by hostile people and a declining economy, others claimed the land as their own and turned cattle loose there to graze.

That all ended late last year. Tolson asked the Kansas attorney general's office for a quitclaim deed to the land, and got it in late October. That meant an end to the grazing, an investigation of the site, and another step in Tolson's journey into remote corners of the state in search of desecrated African American burial sites.

"I've got about eight to 10 sites," said Tolson, who lives in Wichita and who has applied for a $300,000 renewable grant to continue her search. "There's a lot of hidden history here in Kansas. I'm uncovering more all the time."

Norma Tolson's story is the story of a determined woman. Tolson isn't just a coal miner's daughter; she's also a coal miner's granddaughter. Her grandfather owned a coal mine in Weir, which she called one of the most prejudiced little towns you could imagine, a town that made her and other black students march in the back of the line at graduation.

"That's what makes me so determined," Tolson said of that experience and others like it while she was growing up there. "No matter what kind of barrier you have in life, if you're determined, you can succeed."

Determined, she earned an undergraduate degree from Wichita State University, married and had six children, then went back to WSU and earned a master's degree. She later ran a Boeing Wichita training program from her basement and won eight job contracts from the aircraft maker. She employed as many as 80 workers at one point.

About eight years ago, while visiting Weir, she picked up a book about the town's history that had been circulating there. Thumbing through it, she saw little about black residents. "I knew what a contribution they had made," she said. "I owed it to myself and my children and to everyone to tell their story."

By 1997, she was offering readers a book she had published herself: *An Account of Afro-Americans in Weir, Kansas c. 1868-1988.* Telling such stories for people who couldn't do so themselves has become her mission.

During her research, Tolson began hearing from residents of Scammon, a town near Weir, about macabre stories of mass murders and mass burials. Tolson said the story told to her was that in 1899, three streetcars of black miners were sent to Scammon to work in the coal mines. Two of the streetcars were attacked by striking white workers who killed the black men. Their bodies were loaded on wagons and buried in a mass grave. Those in the third streetcar escaped.

After the incident, Tolson said, few people in the community ever spoke about it. In the fall of 2001, preliminary tests done by US Army engineers, who scanned the site south of Scammon for any evidence, were inconclusive. Despite that, a WSU professor said further exploration was needed.

Since then, Tolson has collected volumes of stories and maps of similar burial sites—Flemming, Pittsburg, East Mineral, Critzer.

At yet another site, an entire troop of black soldiers is said to be buried. In one town, someone began building houses over a black cemetery, she said.

Most days she's busy studying maps, ordering microfilm of newspaper articles and firing off e-mail to families who may have lost relatives in the incidents. Sifting the sands of time for whatever granules of truth she can find is painful but necessary. Her determined ears continue to listen for history's shallow breathing and the whispers of a fast fading past.

DON'T OVERLOOK IKE'S CIVIL RIGHTS WORK

February 6, 2004

President Dwight D. Eisenhower presided over our country's postwar innocence of the 1950s, according to most accounts of history, and little more. But David Nichols, dean of faculty emeritus at Southwestern College in Winfield, Kansas, wants you to know that the grandfatherly general most of us know as Abilene's favorite son also was one of the most important presidents on the issue of civil rights in the 20th century.

"Even your most erudite readers, due to the mistakes of historians like Stephen Ambrose, will not believe that Ike was progressive on civil rights," said Nichols, who is writing a book about Eisenhower's civil-rights contributions. "The truth is, he was more progressive than either LBJ or JFK in the '50s."

"The truth is, he was more progressive than either LBJ or JFK in the '50s."

In "Mr. Eisenhower's Civil War: Dwight D. Eisenhower and the struggle for Civil Rights 1953-1961," a book he hopes to finish this year, Nichols said he discusses Earl Warren's appointment to the US Supreme Court following Chief Justice Fred Vinson's death in September 1953. Eisenhower also appointed four other justices to the court, none of them Southerners or segregationists.

Eventually, on May 17, 1954, the court ruled 9-0 to strike down *Plessy v. Ferguson* in the landmark decision known as *Brown v. the Topeka Board of Education* that struck down segregation in public schools. Eisenhower's appointments tipped the scales, making the decision possible.

"The historians have usually superficially made Warren's appointment a political payoff for Warren's support for the presidential nomination, but I believe that is not accurate," Nichols said. "The case had been in the court for some time, and Ike and Attorney General Herbert Brownell knew the decision was coming, and they knew what they were doing in appointing the California governor."

Ike's influence doesn't stop there, Nichols said. Eisenhower appointed E. Frederick Morrow, the first black White House staffer. The president desegregated the District of Columbia, sent troops to Little Rock to enforce the Supreme Court's desegregation order, and, with the urging of Brownell, wrote the 1957 Civil Rights Act, the first such piece of legislation passed since Reconstruction. And while it was President Harry Truman who gave the executive order desegregating the military in 1948, a lot of it still had not happened by the time Ike came into office.

Nichols, who also has written about President Lincoln's Native American policies, cautions against making Ike a saint. He said he has examined the president's administration through a 1950s lens. By today's standards, Eisenhower is a hard sell as a civil-rights warrior. For example, despite his carefully cultivated grandfatherly image, he was known to host stag dinners at the White House, Nichols said. At one such dinner, in the presence of a number of Southern senators, he was heard to say regarding the issue of integration that people were just worried about their daughters consorting with black boys.

Still, Nichols said, Eisenhower's stands on civil rights represented powerful acts of political courage. "The viciousness of racial attitudes was just incredible," Nichols said.

All of this raises the question: If he did so much, why do we know so little about it? Why in the world didn't he speak out? Nichols said it isn't clear why. "He would not do what Kennedy did: raise the issue as a moral issue," Nichols said. "He didn't do his job as a public educator." Even his intervention in Little Rock was less about integration than it was about upholding the Constitution.

Eisenhower never was around black people much, either. He did have black soldiers under his command, but it appears that he may never have resolved his own inner conflict about integration, Nichols said. However, the Civil Rights Act of 1964 and the Voting Rights Act of 1965 were built on the work Eisenhower and Brownell did during the 1950s, Nichols said.

People tend to ignore the 1950s as a sleepy time, Nichols said. But it also was a time of great social awakening in which we learned a new dialect of equality from a quiet man who did much, but spoke little on the subject.

THE LESSONS OF WATERGATE STILL APPLY

June 5, 2005

Having his phone and office bugged at Democratic National Committee headquarters in the early 1970s as a part of the Watergate break-in had a *deja vu* feel to it for Samuel Adams.

Years before, Democratic primaries in his hometown of Waycross, Georgia didn't allow black voters to register, let alone participate. And as a reporter who'd interviewed dozens of civil rights leaders—including Martin Luther King, Jr.—Adams didn't know at the time that the government had tapped his phone.

Each incident is an example of people with power using that power to trample people's rights. "You feel violated being bugged in your own home. You're the target," said Adams, one of my beloved professors in journalism school at the University of Kansas. "(At the DNC) I wasn't the real target."

Sam Adams. Courtesy The Kansas African American Museum.

In the case of Watergate, the real targets, Adams said, were the rights of average citizens who stood between Nixon and the power he sought. Revelations this week about the identity of Deep Throat, the informant who helped topple the Nixon administration, made me think of Adams, who has retired to his native Georgia.

I knew he would have some insights on this, and I wanted to know what he knew and when he knew it.

Adams, who joined the DNC as deputy director of the minorities division in 1971 and later served as associate communications director, said Nixon's exercise of seemingly boundless power over political enemies worried him. And how little one could do against it shocked him.

That Deep Throat turned out to be W. Mark Felt, a 91-year-old former FBI deputy director, also surprised him. He thought that it had to be someone closer to Nixon.

But over the years, he hadn't given the informant's identity much thought.

The symbolism of Nixon's criminal activity, however, did occupy his thoughts. "Being a journalist let me understand politics as one means of social change .... Politics is the exercise of power. Communication is the force that fuels the acceptance of it," Adams said.

But power in our system needs balance, he said. An uncontrolled Democratic Party would have been as bad as an uncontrolled Republican Party. The events surrounding Watergate, he said, tuned him in to trying to get more voters involved in the political process. To empower them so that they could resist the people so brazenly exerting power over their lives. He'd carried that torch for years as a journalist. Adams once posed as a migrant farm worker. By day and under the threat of violence, he adopted the stooped posture and broken speech of the starving, overworked people he'd gone undercover to help. By night, he filed his stories to his editor at *The St. Petersburg* (Florida) *Times*.

He stood only feet away from Alabama governor George Wallace as Wallace attempted to prevent the state's flagship university from integrating. Segregationists chased Adams from restaurants and restrooms—at times at gunpoint—as he tested the impact of the newly passed public accommodations law in each of the formerly Confederate states.

In each case, including his stint at the DNC during the Watergate break-in, there was that same, basic plot of powerful people squeezing less powerful folks. Adams says the best stories always seem to boil down to right and wrong. There's no doubt about which side of the scales he and Felt, whose motives have been questioned, stood on. "You have to be on the side of right," Adams said.

Adams once posed as a migrant farm worker. By day and under the threat of violence, he adopted the stooped posture and broken speech of the starving, overworked people he'd gone undercover to help.

II. Some Were Kings

"Some were paupers, some were kings, and some were masters of their art, but in all their shame, they were all the same, those men with the broken hearts."

—Hank Williams, "Men with Broken Hearts," 1951

WHAT REALLY MATTERS

September 24, 1998

It was a job I initially didn't want. After a stint as a general assignment reporter and a police reporter in Louisville, Kentucky, seven years ago, a job opened in that paper's version of Neighbors. The position offered better hours, more money, and less pressure, but I wasn't sure it was the job for me.

I had been writing stories that I thought really mattered —stories about children trapped in special needs adoption programs, shootings and fatal accidents, and other articles of woe and intrigue. The stories I thought awaited me in the Neighbors section—small town politics, bake sales and bingo—didn't stir my crusading spirit. But soon after taking the job, I learned why such sections really do matter.

Darrell Vanmeter was a freshman at the University of Kentucky, Diana Vanmeter's only child. She was raising him alone. The mother and son lived in a cozy home and were extraordinarily close, almost like inseparable siblings. Darrell regularly scared his mother by hiding under the stairs and playfully grabbing her ankles.

They eked out a life on her modest salary and common sense, and banked their future on his bright promise and driving ambition. Diana was preparing for a weekend of catching up with her son, who was coming home from school that weekend, when she got the call. Darrell had died.

Apparently, Darrell had been suffering from a cold he couldn't shake and instead of staying in bed, he continued to work, to go to class and to volunteer with his fraternity, Phi Beta Sigma. In the middle of one of those hectic days, he collapsed and died during a pick-up basketball game. The daily part of our news operation did a "short"—a sketch of what had happened. "Vanmeter, who was not a member of UK's basketball team, was taken to the Albert B. Chandler

I've often wondered why newspapers sometimes have not made a place for people like Diana and Darrell.

47

Medical Center, but resuscitation efforts failed," read a line in the five-paragraph story.

The cold truth is that sometimes, busy metropolitan papers don't make time for stories like Darrell's. Those stories often slip through the cracks in the daily flurry of politics, policy and priorities. But that's where the Neighbors section comes in.

I wrote about how Darrell had been sick for some time but refused to cancel commitments. I wrote about how the influenza traveled to his heart and eventually stopped it. I quoted friends, relatives and the community he served about how much they would miss him. I told readers that Darrell had his mother's almond eyes. Letters and calls from people moved by the story poured into the paper. The Louisville Chapter of his fraternity held a special memorial in his honor.

But when I saw his mother downtown and opened my mouth to speak, she hurried by, crying. A family member told me later that I reminded her too much of her son.

I've often wondered why newspapers sometimes have not made a place for people like Diana and Darrell. She'd lost her whole world, he was a fantastic kid, and they deserved more than a five-paragraph story. We should make room for everyday people in our news pages, and when we do, sorrowful stories need not fill those spaces exclusively. We want happy stories, too.

We want to know about the kid next door who mows the elderly woman's lawn in the summer and shovels her walk in the winter. Tell us when your child's class takes an interesting field trip to the zoo or to the pumpkin patch to pick out potential jack-o'-lanterns. Call when you think someone's good work in the community has gone unnoticed.

We won't be able to do every story. But September 14, all these years later, I was named team leader for *The Eagle's* Neighbors section, and for the sake of all those stories like Diana's and Darrell's, I'll see to it that we do all those stories that we can. Those stories do matter. They are the absolute essence of what we do.

NIGHTMARE WEIGHS ON FAMILIES OF THE VICTIMS

February 27, 2005

[Note: BTK stands for bind, torture, kill, the acronym used for serial killer Dennis Rader.]

Beyond the congratulatory messages from the state's elite law enforcement officers on what was most assuredly a triumphant moment on a national stage ... Beyond the City Hall south parking lot packed with out-of-town satellite news trucks since the wee hours of the morning ... Beyond the speculation of what may have brought the arrest of a suspect in the city's most notorious serial killings ... Beyond all of that Saturday sat the families of BTK's victims. They joined the cheers as Wichita Police Chief Norman Williams stepped to the microphone and said, "BTK is arrested."

Law enforcement veterans swallowed hard and looked away when asked about their first meeting with the families.

But they'll take a different path to the conclusion than will the rest of us. Many here may consider this mystery solved. District Attorney Nola Foulston has assembled her prosecutorial team. The community can see the end of the paranoia that gripped us for so long, and the beginning of more restful nights. But for the families, the arrest of Dennis Rader means a meandering road. A mixed blessing. A painful journey nearing its end, but a painful journey nonetheless.

Before the opening of the biggest news conference this city has ever seen, cameras lined the walls of the City Council chamber and microphones competed for space atop a City of Wichita podium. Cell phones beeped, buzzed and blared. Journalists mingled with sources and with each other, jockeying for position.

Loud chatter filled the room. But as a somber line of the victims' families moved into the room, down the aisle and into their seats, much of the room fell silent. The weight of what they carried registered on their faces. From the podium, Attorney General Phill Kline spoke eloquently about the life sentences of agony and pain inflicted on them as well as the hope springing from the fact that people cared enough to pursue the person responsible for that agony to the end of justice.

US Representative Todd Tiahrt thanked the faith community who prayed that what was hidden would be revealed and that the victims' families would be uplifted. He said he understood the loss of a loved one, an apparent reference to the suicide of his youngest son, Luke, last July. "I know personally," he said.

Law enforcement veterans swallowed hard and looked away when asked about their first meeting with the families. "I need to think a bit on that one," Chief Williams said. "That was a really intimate time."

Detective Ken Landwehr, the lead investigator on the case, also seemed to gulp, saying only, "That was an emotional time."

Before the news conference, authorities briefed families on the arrest, gave them an opportunity to absorb what had happened, let them decompress.

But as the news conference ended and activity exploded in the room and rolled outside in the hallway, a throng of lights, cameras and microphones lurched toward one of the exits. It resembled the mosh pit at the opening bell of the New York Stock Exchange—people pushing and yelling and waving.

Inside the scrum I could see the stunned face of an elderly woman, Ruth Fox, stepmother of BTK victim Nancy Fox. She no doubt wanted to leave, but she couldn't. That's where all of those families will live for awhile, wanting to escape it, but being confronted with the fact that they'll have to fight through it.

They live among us, but forever live set apart. Rise and sleep next door as neighbors, but engage in a struggle far from anything most of us could imagine. They live more intensely the nightmare we all shared.

ONE LESS WEAPON FOR ABUSERS

September 11, 2005

You don't see razor strops much anymore. They used to hang in nearly every barber shop. Barbers used razor strops—2-foot-long, roughly 3-inch-wide double-layered strips of leather—to sharpen shaving blades. I almost never think about them. But then again, no one ever hit me with one. If someone had, it likely wouldn't have taken a speech to stir the memory of the first time I saw a razor strop.

A woman I'll call Erin, who said she escaped an oppressive relationship, spoke powerfully at a Choose Respect domestic violence prevention rally last month featuring former Syracuse University and NFL quarterback Don McPherson. McPherson was great, but Erin stole the show.

She shared painful stories of how, to avoid a beating, she trained herself to stare at the dashboard of the car as she rode with her ex-husband because he'd accuse her of looking at another man if she looked out the window. How that ex-husband intimidated her out of flashing the dazzling smile that earned her an award in elementary school. How she once sent her son next door to call the police or get help during an argument, only to later find the boy sitting in the garage, frightened, because he'd also been taught not to talk to strangers. The neighbors were strangers, she said, because her husband forbade any of them to talk to anyone.

When I spoke to her briefly after her presentation, I told her that the fear and desperation in her story had dug up an old memory. When I was 7, some friends and I were playing in the yard when a frantic woman came running toward us, begging us to hide her. A brawny man carrying a razor strop in his meaty hands stepped out of a car just after we hid her.

When he asked if we'd seen a woman come running by, I was so scared I could barely breathe. I remember looking

But razor strops weren't used only to straighten out blades. They were used to straighten out people, too, mostly children and sometimes women.

at the strop and thinking that I wouldn't hit a dog with that thing, let alone a person. As I stared, the older kids with me shook their heads "no" to the man's question. He tossed his razor strop in the seat, jumped back into the car and sped away.

Razor strops are heavy. They sharpen and straighten out blades. During regular use, blade edges can bend, even curl. But razor strops weren't used only to straighten out blades. They were used to straighten out people, too, mostly children and sometimes women. Women like the one we hid.

Erin said she'd had a similar experience as a child. In her case, a terrified woman burst through her family's front door saying that a man was chasing her with a gun. Erin said her mother hid the woman and called the police.

As I thought about my razor strop memory, I realized that I hadn't seen one of those strops in years. I found a few barbers who explained how razor strops had worn out their usefulness. Barbers who shave customers today use disposable blades instead of constantly brushing the blade on the strop. And given the fears of blood-borne virus transmission—from the blade to the strop to the blade to a new customer—the strops aren't sanitary, either.

Basically, enlightenment and invention have made them obsolete. Now, about the only place a nonprofessional will find razor strops is on websites that sell them as antiques. Pieces of American nostalgia. Collectibles. You really don't see razor strops that much anymore. And perhaps, given the way some people have misused them, that's for the best.

Losing a Job Can Prompt a Dive into Desperation*

May 25, 2005

Behold, life's treadmill—work, then home. Paycheck, bills. Work, then home. Paycheck, bills. A modest pace, but terrible monotony. If you walk faster, it continues. Was Bennie Herring on such a treadmill? Did he fall off last December when he lost his job? Plodding along on the treadmill can seem difficult enough. It never stops, step after step. Eventually, what has been easy becomes laborious.

But what happens when you fall, when you lose your job? When that question, that awful question, begins to tickle your subconscious: "What am I going to do?"

How could he hold so much turmoil inside and no one know?

Do you, as Kansas City police say Herring did more than a week ago, walk into a bank wearing a dark ski mask and camouflage pants? How could it be that this man— whom most people described as elegant, refined, reflective—stands charged with staging a bizarre, daylight bank robbery?

How could this man, who didn't even own a gun, this 44-year-old man with beloved pet birds chirping in his immaculate home, be accused of holding a gun to someone's head? Stripping hostages to their underwear? Demanding a plane?

Had he fallen off the treadmill of work, then home, paycheck, bills? Losing work may have meant no home, no paycheck, no way to pay bills. How could he hold so much turmoil inside and no one know? Would it equate with simply not reacting as a heavy, crushing machine snags your shirt and slowly pulls you in? Instinct says fight, flap, flail as the whirring teeth of the machine drag you closer.

And yet, Herring apparently hid that desperation. Pushed it down. One of the bank employees said in an interview on ABC's *Good Morning America* last week that the robber moved with stoic efficiency through each phase of the holdup. "It looked like he knew the police were there the entire time, and he was taking his time," the employee told the news show. "There was no rush, no excitement, no nothing."

Back in Wichita, according to *The Eagle,* Herring's family and friends have scoured his life and apartment for a hint at why. "Everything in the apartment was normal," said Brad Cooper, pastor of Cross Road Fellowship Bible Church. "There's nothing." Perhaps, as Henry David Thoreau said, "the mass of men lead lives of quiet desperation." What is called resignation, he said, is confirmed desperation. Everyone has a tipping point, it seems. Many other Wichitans looked into that abyss last week and saw their reflection.

Will they don a mask, buy a pistol and knock off a bank? Probably not. Most of us pounding away on our treadmills understand that we can't do that, no matter how desperate we become. But can you imagine the desperation at kitchen tables Saturday morning as Boeing Wichita employees waited for a letter telling them if they should even bother getting up Monday morning? And that awful question. "What am I going to do?" The same question Herring may have been asking himself when he lost his job. When he couldn't contain his desperation. When he fell from life's treadmill.

But can you imagine the desperation at kitchen tables Saturday morning as Boeing Wichita employees waited for a letter telling them if they should even bother getting up Monday morning?

WHY ISN'T MAN'S DEATH AFFECTING MORE OF US?

January 23, 2005

A man died here last week. Just thought you ought to know. The media reported his death early in the week. Since then, I've heard very little about him. No public outcry. Nothing much to indicate he's gone. The realization that this death barely registered with most of us seems worse than the humble circumstances of his death.

Once upon a time, a death like this one would have shamed us.

Someone found him in a van just before noon Monday. Temperatures the night before had plunged to 16 degrees. Neighbors said it was not uncommon for the man to sleep in the van when he had nowhere else to stay.

He's gone, and at the most critical juncture of life, where this life ends and another begins, all we know about him would fit on a Post-it note. Some of that is journalistic custom. We don't immediately name people who die. I just wish we all—including me—had done or said more. More than his name, Randall "Randy" Taylor. More than his age, 47. More than the general location of his death, somewhere in the 1700 block of South Waco.

I thought at least a few people would call Opinion Line, *The Eagle's* barometer for public outrage, and lament how anonymously people die anymore, even when they die in a very public way. But I didn't see much of that, nor did I get a sense from anyone about who he was. No clue where he worshipped, if he did. Did he ever have a child? Or a wife? What did he do for a living once upon a time? Did anyone care? I'm sure some people did.

I saw the look in the Rev. Sam Muyskens' eyes during a television interview after the man's body was discovered. I've met Muyskens, executive director of Inter-Faith Ministries, which champions homeless causes. He's solid. Composed. But the expression on his face and the way his words tumbled out spoke to how deeply this affected him.

How it should affect all of us.

I can remember being a little boy holding tight to my father's arm as we navigated sleeping bodies on a sidewalk in downtown Los Angeles. These men seemed huge to me. They wore layers of soiled clothing. They reeked of alcohol as well as misery. They slept under newspapers and rags. I was afraid of them.

Sensing that, my father shared a poem that I've never forgotten. I don't know the author. All I know is that it helped me begin to understand not simply the pain of homelessness, but also the cruel turns life can take: "Some were paupers, some were kings, and some were masters of their art, but in all their shame, they were all the same, those men with the broken hearts." Just broken people who may have had little but a life full of suffering.

Now that we know how he died, we will get busy forgetting.

A life was here and now is gone. I called and wanted to know where he was. Where he might end up. What kind of burial he'd get, if any. The coroner's office's preliminary determination was that the man died from natural disease and exposure, which means the cold at least contributed to his death.

As if that matters. Even if the cold had not killed him, this man slept in a van on a night so cold people brought their dogs inside. Now that we know how he died, we will get busy forgetting. Lives flare and fade like matches anymore. Once upon a time, a death like this one would have shamed us. Not anymore, it seems.

This isn't necessarily a plea for more help, although that would be great. It's simply a question: Why don't we seem to care? It has been bitterly cold outside in the last couple of weeks, but our hearts must be much colder when this kind of tragedy barely sends a ripple through our collective conscience.

A man died here Monday in a freezing van. Just thought you ought to know.

TIME MEANINGLESS WITHOUT FRIENDS

October 10, 2003

I never seem to have time for much of anything beyond work during the week. I'm at work before anything opens and often getting home long after everything else has closed. That's why Saturdays are so special. That's my time to relax with family. To run errands. To finally cut the yard after all those days of rain. To read. To travel. To catch a good game.

I'd certainly have traded all of my Saturdays for this particular friend.

Last Saturday, though, a frightening call interrupted my routine. One of my best friends, Van Williams, whom most of you will know for his work here at *The Eagle* simultaneously covering and uncovering City Hall, had been rushed to the hospital. No one seemed to know the prognosis.

Van had been running in that weekend's Corporate Challenge, a friendly athletic competition between the business giants in town benefiting local charities. Not far into the race, he felt a peculiar sensation buzzing in the back of his head. As he's apt to do, he forged ahead. Hard work is his cure-all. But the pain continued to grow until he had to stop a fellow runner and ask for immediate help.

A kind soul, whom we still haven't found, scooped him into her van and rushed him to Wesley Medical Center, where tests showed that a blood vessel had burst. By that time, more than two dozen family members, friends and co-workers had taken over the waiting room.

His generous spirit had brought us there. Whenever I tell people about him, I emphasize his best quality: He's such a good friend that whenever something good happens to you, he's more excited about it than you are.

"Is he famous?" Van's stepfather, a tall, soft-spoken man, told me that other families seemed puzzled by the number and variety of people camped out in the waiting room of the hospital's medical intensive-care unit as if they were guarding a demilitarized zone. Black people, white people, Mexican-Americans. Pensive seniors and busy toddlers logged long hours there, too uncomfortable to relax at home knowing that Van was in trouble. "Is he famous?" they asked. "Who is he?"

The outpouring has been amazing. During a short visit I made to his room this week, he got calls from Milwaukee and Las Vegas and had four visitors, each quietly urging the fates to let him stay and laugh with us a little while longer.

I'm relieved that doctors have moved him out of ICU and into a regular room. He's not completely out of the woods, but if he rests (something he finds difficult to do), he should be fine. As I sat in his room with his wife, his mother and his sister the other night, it occurred to me that I'd spent somewhere close to 30 hours at the hospital praying for his recovery. I'd hardly noticed the passage of time. I guess time is meaningless without friends. I'd certainly have traded all of my Saturdays for this particular friend.

UNLIKE RUSH, LORD'S DINER DOESN'T JUDGE

November 21, 2004

Wendy Glick sees life in circles. Circles that link every human being. Circles that surround and protect. Circles that mark our paths through life sometimes. Even the social circles we move in. "You know what you live," says Glick, director of The Lord's Diner downtown, meaning people too often observe the world in all of its breadth from inside their own insular world.

That's why she seemed so patient in her response to radio rube Rush Limbaugh, who recently implied that some of the people waiting in those long lines every night at The Lord's Diner didn't really need the free meal the diner provides. Reading an *Eagle* report, Limbaugh mocked Glick, who had said that new families showing up for help looked uncomfortable. "They're wondering if they're going to get away with it, Wendy," Limbaugh said on air. Rush could learn a thing or two from Glick. "First of all," Glick says, "I think it's awesome that Rush Limbaugh reads *The Wichita Eagle*. But The Lord's Diner is here to serve, not to judge."

People have more than one kind of hunger, she said. People hunger for fellowship as well as food. Some people come to the diner terribly lonely and hungry, and they get nourished in the way they need to be nourished. Maybe Limbaugh found himself scrambling for program material and thought the diner an easy target. Maybe he's so tied to ideology that he can't bring himself to admit that the economy is bad and people are hurting. Or maybe it was just the OxyContin talking.

That last comment might seem like a cheap shot. Limbaugh admitted on his radio program last year that he'd been addicted to the painkiller since an unsuccessful back surgery and later hired lawyers to keep his medical records sealed. But a rich talk radio host bashing poor people who

Maybe Limbaugh found himself scrambling for program material and thought the diner an easy target.

can't afford lawyers to hide their pharmacological pecca-dilloes is pretty doggone sorry, too.

As I said, he could learn a lot from Glick, who, a few years ago, began living a larger life. After selling off her Skate East and Skate South businesses, and as she says, doing the stay-at-home-mom thing, Glick felt her faith pulling her into volunteering for Catholic Charities, which serves the poor.

There, she formed her own part of the circle with people outside her usual orbit. And they notice when she's styled her hair differently and they think enough of her to tell her. They smile and thank her constantly. They see fatigue in her eyes and encourage her to please go home and rest.

She said, having been tucked away in an east-side com-munity, she had no idea of the need in our community. "If you don't live it, you just don't know it," she said. "Just a lack of knowledge." Now she's so in tune that she can watch a family standing in the food line and tell they are there for the first time because they don't know the pro-cedure. They're holding documents that other charities require before helping anyone. But The Lord's Diner re-quires no such documents. All you have to do is sign in.

And as welcoming as the staff at the diner tries to be, it still can be very humbling to stand in line for food, Glick said. "I just wish that he (Limbaugh) could make statements with more knowledge," adding that she'd gotten a contribu-tion Wednesday in his honor. "I invite anyone who'd like to see The Lord's Diner to come on down for dinner."

I think Rush should visit and live something he doesn't know. He should stand in line with the people for whom The Lord's Diner exists as the most benevolent of bless-ings. Sit with them and tell them that they're freeloaders. Step out of his glass-encased recording booth into a new, larger world. One that begins and ends with individuals, people to whom we're all linked.

9/11 FAMILIES SHOULD STOP GRIPING

January 9, 2004

As architect Michael Arad unveiled his design of the World Trade Center memorial this week to boos and criticism, my mind drifted to an anniversary that will come and go this month with hardly any notice.

Nearly 40 years ago, a KC-135, swollen with fuel, fell out of the cold January sky and slammed into a sleeping neighborhood near 21st and Piatt. Within a few seconds of the crash, 14 adults—including a pregnant woman whose unborn child usually is counted as the 30th victim of the crash—and eight children died, along with the seven-member crew. Two families were wiped out. Twenty-six people were injured.

Seven houses were reduced to smoking rubble. More than 65 houses were so badly damaged that residents could not stay there; 50 more were less seriously damaged. The impact of the crash left a 15-foot-deep crater in the vacant lot behind what was then Razook's Thriftway Supermarket at 21st and Piatt, and drove the tanker's engines 6 feet underground.

I lost my maternal grandmother, Mary Daniels; an uncle, C.L. Daniels; and a 5-year-old cousin, Tracy Randolph, a kindergartner at Washington Elementary School. Local newspaper accounts wept with earnest grief. An editorial titled "When tragedy strikes" scolded people as "callous" who trolled the blighted area for souvenirs. It also asked the larger community "to do all that is possible to help the victims and their families. Let us continue to show that we are a community with heart."

Today, a playground and plaque mark the site, and surviving family members quietly went on with their lives, though always hurting from their losses. I have a hard time imagining any of them complaining about this communi-

The families of the men and women killed in Afghanistan and Iraq while trying to prevent future terrorist attacks certainly won't collect million-dollar checks.

ty's earnest efforts to help them manage all that grief, about whether the park and memorial sufficiently captured the moment, or about the modest financial settlements. That's why I found the criticism of the trade center memorial by surviving family members so disturbing.

"Reflecting Absence" will memorialize the victims of the 9/11 attacks and the six people killed in the 1993 trade center bombing. It will be one of two focal points at the trade center site, along with the 1,776-foot glass skyscraper known as the Freedom Tower. But surviving family members have said the design doesn't help people understand the attack that destroyed the trade center. "None of the designs are up to par," said Anthony Gardner, a member of a coalition for 9/11 family groups. "They don't communicate the enormity."

This follows other complaints from family members about federal settlements averaging $1.6 million offered in exchange for not filing wrongful-death suits against the airlines. They're hurting, and that's easy to understand. But they're acting as if they are the only people in the world who've ever lost a loved one to tragedy. Somehow they've come to believe the memorial belongs only to them.

The 9/11 attacks touched us all—if not through agonizing hours of dialing and redialing into busy signals in an attempt to reach loved ones in the crumbled twin towers, then through the ever-present thoughts that maybe it can happen here. And since when does someone owe us something when we lose a loved one? The families of the men and women killed in Afghanistan and Iraq while trying to prevent future terrorist attacks certainly won't collect million-dollar checks. And as controversial as this war has become, US soldiers may never get a memorial honoring their brave service.

I understand why letting go can prove so difficult. I realized only this year just how much my aunt, who lost her 5-year-old in that plane crash, suffered during the 30 years following the crash. She smothered my sister's two sons in hugs and clothes and toys. She did the same with me and a number of my cousins. My sister says my aunt likely gravitated to my nephews, my cousins and me because, as little boys, we didn't remind her of the little girl she'd lost.

She died in February 1995, and I can't remember her ever complaining that someone owed her for the loss of her child. And here we have people complaining about our society funding a multimillion-dollar memorial and million-dollar settlements? My God. Whatever happened to "thank you"?

FAMILY TRIES TO COPE AFTER INMATE'S DEATH

March 28, 2006

At a tidy little house on North Ash on Monday, cars lined the driveway and the street. Visitors walked in and out, some of them tearful. Some chatted with a tiny little girl who doesn't know what has happened.

Danielle Morris invited me in. She's 23 and remarkably calm a day after the death of her father, Alexis Mc-Cullough, an inmate at the work release center downtown. A witness and friend in the next bed said he died after hours of begging for help. Danielle's newborn slept in one room, while the family scurried about in the next room, digging through a box of photographs for a photo fit for an obituary.

This is the scene people don't see. The other side. The scene of people grappling with a loss of someone like Danielle's dad, the best way they can. He'd landed in work release following arson and robbery convictions. Maybe, they wondered, he was the kind of man no one thought was important enough to listen to until it was too late.

Activity swirls around Danielle. Calls from me. Calls from television stations. Could we borrow a photo? Suddenly, people are paying attention. Everyone wants to talk now, she thought. Why not Sunday morning? Where was everyone then? Sunday was when her father's friend and fellow inmate, Andre Anderson, called to tell her that her dad was sweating, struggling to breathe and crying out in pain. "You need to call them and tell them to get some help for your dad," she said Anderson told her.

> *When she called, she said the person who answered seemed more interested in which inmate had called Danielle.*

When she called, she said the person who answered seemed more interested in which inmate had called Danielle. "Who called you?" the person asked. Who called is irrelevant, she said she told the person on the other end of the phone. She said the person at the work release center told her that nothing could be done until Monday. But the calls from Anderson and at least three other inmates continued. He needs help. He's getting worse. About three hours after her first phone call to the work release center, her father, the man she'll remember as playful and protective, died.

An official investigation is under way, said Bill Miskell, interim public information officer for the state Department of Corrections. Miskell said McCullough saw a doctor last week and saw a nurse Sunday. He said he couldn't say much more until after the investigation. But that investigation meant that her father's body temporarily belonged to the state, that she couldn't see him until after an autopsy.

Is it really him, she thought? How would we know if we can't see him? What rights do we have? Anderson told her, "I hate to say it like this, but the way your dad died, you wouldn't want to see it. He suffered. They watched him die."

And so, a family grieves. People stop by to comfort each other. They look for a photograph that suitably tells the story of his life. And a 23-year-old daughter with a new baby tries to answer reporters' questions while her own questions mount: Is this what it means to be thought of as someone who doesn't matter? Why wouldn't anyone believe him? Why didn't they call an ambulance? Why did her father have to die days short of his 42nd birthday, begging for his life?

PARKS DESERVES STATUS HE DIDN'T RECEIVE IN LIFE

March 8, 2006

His contributions weren't black contributions. He was truly a citizen of the world.

Now that Gordon Parks—the most important Kansan since President Eisenhower or Alf Landon—has died, I hope we will praise him. I have difficulty understanding how so many people, Kansans especially, didn't know the breadth of his influence. But maybe now that he's gone, we'll embrace this great photographer, filmmaker and author. This great man.

"Now that he's safely dead, let us praise him," wrote Carl Hines, Jr. in "A Dead Man's Dream," about Martin Luther King, Jr. "Build monuments to his glory, sing hosannas to his name."

Building monuments is definitely something that Wichita didn't do while Parks was alive. His passing fills me not only with sadness, but also with regret. Regret that a majority of the Wichita City Council, in order to save a few dollars per square foot on the cost of a library, voted years ago not to build a museum within a library to house his art. Regret that Wichita State University didn't keep the collection he offered. The art now is owned by the Corcoran Gallery in Washington, D.C.

Regret that our community, including the Kansas African American Museum, didn't push harder for a fundraising campaign for a new building that was to feature his genius, his contributions and perhaps even his name.

I can't shake this profound sadness about how too few of us knew about the deep mark he left on this world. After learning of Parks' death early Tuesday evening, I started checking websites. *The Eagle's* site, Kansas.com, reported it. So did *USA Today.* But CNN listed it eighth, below stories about Google's stock, Dana Reeve's death and a

Right: Gordon Parks at home.
Courtesy The Kansas African American Museum.

66

Toni Parks
© Nyc 1990

new book about Major League Baseball star Barry Bonds' alleged steroid use.

Consider his difficult start in life in Fort Scott: loss, racism, and poverty, all heartache detailed in his best-known written work, *The Learning Tree*. His lesson to us was his choice of weapons, a phrase he also used as the title of one of his autobiographical works. His choice of weapons was his photographic eye, his canvas of words, his soaring intellect. With those weapons, Parks taught the world about the power of ideas and images to shape souls and harbor hopes in a sometimes soulless and hopeless world.

He spent his most important years painting pictures of desperate poverty, from American ghettos to sprawling South American slums. In each place, he used his weapons of choice to share a message about how best to confront the cruelties of life. Despite his undeniable brilliance, you never got the sense that he hungered for the spotlight. In fact, a strand of humility and quiet dignity runs through his life and through his work. He came from nothing but, by hard work and perseverance, touched millions through his prolific pen, lightning shutter and cinematic power. We haven't seen a more quintessential Kansan.

And yet, his writings aren't required reading in schools here, despite their timeless messages. And yet, only pockets of people here and there seem to truly appreciate his towering work.

And yet. That's what I'm left with after learning of his death: And yet. And yet ... His contributions weren't black contributions. He was truly a citizen of the world. My prayer is that he achieves in death the status that he truly deserved but didn't sufficiently and rightfully receive in life. That is my hope, even though Hines cautioned in his poem that "Dead men make such convenient heroes. They cannot rise to challenge the images we fashion from their lives and besides, it's easier to build monuments than to make a better world." Parks was one of the few of us who could actually say he made the world a better place. So, finally, let the praises begin.

NEGLECTED, PARKS' STORY IS HISTORY LOST

November 2, 2005

America lost Rosa Parks long before she passed away last week. Maybe even years ago. We lost her because we didn't protect her, literally and figuratively. When you don't protect something, you lose it. That's true for people, possessions, relationships.

It is difficult to recall someone other than Mrs. Parks who sacrificed so much for people only to suffer so publicly. Given what she endured in recent years in popular culture and personally, the treatment she got from the Alabama segregationists—who arrested and prosecuted her in 1955 for refusing to give up her bus seat to a white man—must have felt downright cozy.

You couldn't pay me a million dollars, for example, to be Cedric the Entertainer or anyone else associated with the movie *Barbershop*, now that Mrs. Parks is gone. He must feel terrible. "Rosa Parks ain't do nothing but sit her [#@&] down," Cedric says in the film.

Nothing, huh? Nothing but live an upstanding life. Nothing but live an involved life for the sake of her community and the nation's credibility. Nothing but suffer a lot of indignities so your ignorant [#@&] could use one of the rare cinematic opportunities black folks have to say something like that. She settled a case last year with the Grammy Award-winning rap duo OutKast for exploiting her image to sell songs.

In 1994, a drug addict kicked in the door of her downtown Detroit apartment, beat her and robbed her of $53. And in 2002 her landlord threatened to evict her from her high-rise apartment after her caregivers missed rental payments. In October 2004, they opted to let her live there rent-free permanently.

At each point I can remember trying to figure out why

> *You couldn't pay me a million dollars, for example, to be Cedric the Entertainer or anyone else associated with the movie* **Barbershop,** *now that Mrs. Parks is gone.*

this was happening. How we allowed such things to happen to her. Why we weren't protecting her.

A 2003 article in the *Christian Science Monitor* gave me a hint."Rosa Parks' legacy is in danger," said Doreen Loury, a professor of African American studies at Arcadia University in Philadelphia, in the *Monitor.* "Not because

Rosa Parks getting arrested, US Government photo.

of its mention in popular movies and song, but because so few Americans who can recognize the great lady's face on a poster have any idea what legal, political, and personal struggles put her there."

I'm not certain how something like this happens, but I suspect that it has a lot to do with how history gets sanitized, diluted, sweetened and rendered one-dimensional or unimportant. A lot of people here can remember, for example, when black women in Wichita had to take clothing home to try it on because they weren't allowed in dressing rooms in downtown clothing stores. When theaters were segregated. When swimming pools were drained after black people swam in them so white swimmers wouldn't have to backstroke in the same water.

But depictions of that era get neutered. Tidied up. Sugar-coated.

Without the depth, perspective gets lost, and that's how we end up with fools saying Mrs. Parks didn't do anything but sit on a bus. I'm still nauseated by the thought of a black filmmaker introducing such a blasphemous sentiment in his film. We've got to be more careful with history. Protect it. If we don't, we'll lose it. The way we lost Mrs. Parks, a long time ago.

THE EMPTY SPACE THAT'S LEFT BEHIND

December 2, 2005

After I scored my only high school touchdown, I can remember my coach asking on the team bus, "Did you have any family here to see it?" I was able to say yes. As I walked off the field at Carpenter Stadium at South High, I saw my cousin Gary Holloway standing at the fence, smiling and telling me way to go.

That someone who knew me, a family member who'd watched me grow up, had been there to share that moment.

I hadn't realized he was there, and I'm still not sure why he was. He never told me that he was coming to watch me play. That he never said anything about it said a lot about him. Some folks need credit for every little thing they do. At least in my case, Gary didn't.

Despite my coach teasing me that I ran so slowly after catching the ball that it looked as though I was pushing a plow down a muddy field, I felt enormously proud that Gary was there. That someone who knew me, a family member who'd watched me grow up, had been there to share that moment.

I didn't realize just how much a part of my life he'd been until our family lost him the Saturday after Thanksgiving. Gary died in his sleep, at home here in Wichita. He was 51. I can't recall any phone calls between us and I don't remember us hanging out much. We didn't have too many of those tender moments that form the boundaries of close relationships.

But I saw him at every family gathering and at the construction company office where he worked as an estimator with his brothers and cousins. I also remember him graduating from Emporia State University. Others in the family had earned degrees, but he was the first college graduate I actually can remember. He wore a black gown and mortarboard, smiling his broad smile.

The first time I went to St. Louis, it was because I'd

traveled there with a busload of our family to see him get married. I've always associated St. Louis with him. My first trip to the Gateway Arch, seeing old Busch Stadium. Touring a huge town filled with history. Those experiences changed me. Sort of like that Saturday morning.

His brothers and sister hadn't heard him stirring as usual and his brother went into the basement to check on him. Unable to wake him, one of his brothers shook him and shook him, pleading with him to wake up. When my sister called me in Memphis, where I was visiting other family, my eyes stung and my mind began to tear through the impossibility of Gary being gone. Gary? Gone? Can this be happening? Gary was always supposed to be there.

But now, there's a hole there we can only fill with memories. This column is about Gary, but it's also about people like him—the fixtures in our lives we too often assume always will be there. I'd never known a time in my life when he wasn't there.

That's the pain we feel dealing with the loss of someone whom we never considered having to do without. The people who take the time to cheer us on from the stands of life when we don't even know they're there. People who support us and fill giant spaces in our lives. People who leave giant holes in us, in our lives, when they're gone.

RESPECT FOR LIFE MISSING IN A VIDEO OF DEATH

July 3, 2007

As stabbing victim LaShanda Calloway lay bleeding on the floor of a convenience store at 25th Street North and Hillside, no fewer than five store patrons stepped over her to complete purchases—and at least one took cell phone pictures of her—before bothering to call 911, police said.

Police have been told that some of those photos landed on the Internet. "It's on the video," said Wichita Police Chief Norman Williams. "She laid on the floor while people continued to do their shopping. They're taking photographs. That's our frustration. They didn't call immediately. If people would have been calling us, who knows what the outcome might have been." Calloway, who was stabbed after an altercation June 23, eventually died at the hospital from her injuries.

A witness questioned last week whether a policy that prevents fire crews from entering potentially violent situations until police have secured the site contributed to Calloway's death. He said he and others frantically waved to the firefighters to come and help, but they didn't move in until a Highway Patrol cruiser entered the parking lot.

Yet Calloway lost approximately two precious minutes while patrons strangely ignored her, according to Wichita Police Spokesman Gordon Bassham. "This is one of the most disgusting examples of disregard for life I've ever seen," Bassham said of the video. "It is a very, very tragic video to watch. It was revolting to see this lack of humanity."

The video showed the 27-year-old Calloway struggling to her feet and collapsing three times without anyone helping her. Worse, one woman who stepped over Calloway four times while shopping, eventually paused to snap a photo of her with a cell phone.

And now, police are trying to track down photos of a dying Calloway that someone told them had been posted on the Internet. "This is just appalling," Williams said. "I could continue shopping and not render aid and then take time out to take a picture? That's crazy. What happened to our respect for life?"

Fatima Kazia, who co-owns the Noori Convenience store at 2601 North Hillside with her husband, said that she doesn't believe her employee saw the stabbing or saw Calloway lying on the floor. "Our mind is on the customer in front of us," Kazia said. "Sometimes we can't see what they (customers) are doing." If her employee had seen something, he would have told her or her husband, Kazia said. The employee has since quit.

Two people—Cherish M. McCullough and George R. Brown—turned themselves in to police and were arrested in connection with the death. I'm wondering, though, if the people who so callously stepped over Calloway could face some sort of punishment. "The only possible charge that could conceivably be filed is a failure to render aid, and that's a DA (district attorney's) call," Bassham said.

Williams said most people do call 911 in these situations. Still, it's not as unusual as you might think for people to wait to call police or EMS. "This is concerning," Williams said. "This is one of those infrequent things that we see, people calling their friends to report things before calling 911. It is infrequent, but it does happen, and it is frustrating to us in law enforcement because time is of the essence. People need to call immediately."

And they need to call 911, instead of calling up their cell phone's camera function.

Worse, one woman who stepped over Calloway four times while shopping, eventually paused to snap a photo of her with a cell phone.

THE ONLY PEACE IS A PAINFUL ONE

November 16, 2005

Cassie Boone says she doesn't deserve any recognition, any acknowledgment, anything for sitting with a dying 23-year-old man who had just been thrown from his motorcycle.

At first, she asked that I not use her name in this column. "I don't want any appreciation for it," she said through tears. "I couldn't save him. I don't feel like I deserve anything. I don't want people to talk to me about it." She wants the tears to stop, and she wants to share the young man's last words with his mother. "He wanted me to tell his mom that he loved her," she said.

Maybe it was because Wes was so close to her age. Maybe because she'd once lost a friend in a motorcycle accident.

Cassie was driving home from her own mother's house Saturday night on 1-235 when suddenly, traffic slowed. She saw someone standing in the roadway directing cars. Then she saw a motorcycle piled up on the side of the road and a young man, beyond the shoulder, beyond the guardrail, lying on his stomach on a patch of sloping grass. Cassie said she ran to him. She'd taken a CPR class and thought she might be able to help, to comfort and stabilize him until help arrived.

But he was badly wounded, she said, and his legs and back appeared to be broken. She kneeled over him, putting one hand on his neck to take his pulse. She rubbed circles on his back with her other hand. While another motorist called for help, Cassie opened his wallet to figure out his name: Abram Wesley "Wes" Christopher. Born March 12, 1982.

She'd learn later that he went to school in Protection and graduated from Ashland High School in 2000. That he'd earned an associate's degree in liberal arts from Hutchinson Community College and attended Wichita State University. That he was a member of First Christian Church in Protection.

Cassie said she tried to keep Wes calm, but he was in a lot of pain. Then he started shaking. That's when he said, "Tell my mom I love her." "He was just very scared," she said. She continued rubbing circles on his back and, for a moment, he appeared to relax. But she realized that his pulse had slowed. And then it stopped.

When the police arrived, they asked everyone who didn't see the accident to please leave, so she did. But the image of that moment didn't leave her. "I dream about it," said Cassie, 20. "It takes me a long time to go to sleep. I see it when I close my eyes. I get so upset."

Maybe it was because Wes was so close to her age. Maybe because she'd once lost a friend in a motorcycle accident. Maybe it had something to do with her walking away from a nursing career, after completing some of the basic courses, because she didn't think she could stand the sight of blood. "I don't like to talk about it," she said, her tears returning. "I cry whenever I do."

Cassie said her mother suffered right along with her at first, unsure how to help. But then her mother counseled her on how Cassie might try to find Wes' mother and his family. To let them know about the last moments of his life. Cassie tore into the phone book. She called in search of the law officers who worked the accident. She called media. She called funeral homes. But she couldn't find Wes' mother.

And inside, she wondered whether she really wanted to. She was torn. She couldn't imagine what it must be like to lose a child. Would talking about Wes help? What if talking wasn't something that his family wanted to do? "But that's what he wanted me to do," she said. She couldn't save Wes. Couldn't comfort him much, either. But if she could somehow honor his dying wish, maybe that's comfort enough.

OPPOSITION TO GAY MARRIAGE FUELED BY HATE

February 6, 2005

Don't use God to justify hate. Hate is ugly, and God don't like ugly.

President Bush's state of the union comments about banning same-sex marriage, as well as the Kansas Legislature's decision to put the issue to a public vote, travel to us as an ugly echo from a dark and not-so-distant past.

Too many people in our country can't seem to function without a scapegoat. If it's not black people, it's Jewish people. If it's not Jewish people, it's Hispanic people. If it's not Hispanic people it's gay people, and if it's not gay people, it's so-called liberals.

In each instance, the perpetrators cloak their hate and fear in the Stars and Stripes, in the robes of religion, or both, with frightening results. Once upon a time in this country, an ideology separated the races based on a deep and unspeakable fear: that black men and white women might "know" each other, in the biblical sense.

This ideology existed almost exclusively to protect white womanhood. I say that because white men, from Thomas Jefferson to Senator Strom Thurmond, didn't seem to have any problems with race mixing as long as white men were doing the mixing.

That's why two men dragged 14-year-old Emmett Till out of bed, crushed his skull, shot him in the head and tossed him into the Tallahatchie River after he'd talked fresh to a white woman. That's why President Woodrow Wilson screened D.W. Griffith's *Birth of a Nation* at the White House. In the film, a vengeful Ku Klux Klan rescues white society from black men seething with lust for white women. Wilson said the movie represented "history written with lightning" and was "all so terribly true."

That's why mobs lynched black men who may or may not have looked too long or spoken with too much familiarity to a white woman. That's why society segregated schools, hospitals, neighborhoods, restaurants. All of this based on ugly, ignorant and imagined fear that people believed God sanctioned. That's why worshippers of this ideology burned crosses. They weren't desecrating the cross; they sought to illuminate the spirit of Christ in this dark world of sinfulness.

So this notion from the president and from legislators about protecting the sacred institution of marriage—by denying some people rights—exudes a haunting familiarity. Marriages fail for many reasons. Because one spouse saves and the other one spends. Because of drug abuse. Because of infidelity. Because of meddling in-laws. Because one heats up slowly like a crock pot and the other like a microwave.

I doubt that a gay or lesbian couple's marriage even makes the list of the top 100 things we need to do to protect marriage. So let's call this amendment what it really is: fear mongering. Our legislature actually took up the process of funding our under-funded school system after debating this ridiculous amendment. Let's protect children from the people who bite and shake them to death or keep them in basements instead of denying gay people rights promised by the constitution—the right to life, liberty and the pursuit of happiness.

If you choose to believe that gay and lesbian people choose their sexual orientation despite everything they say to the contrary, then that's your right. If you choose to believe the increased visibility of gay and lesbian people represents a slide in our moral values, if you choose to believe that people want to mainstream aberrant behavior, that, too, is your right.

I say let God sort it out. God wasn't guilty of creative malfeasance when he breathed life into us. He loves us all, every one, whether any of us choose to love each other or not.

Don't use God to justify hate. Hate is ugly, and God don't like ugly.

THIS KU FAN FINDS IT HARD TO BE HUMBLED

March 22, 2006

I said it, but I'm not proud of it. I didn't really mean it. In fact, I'll be cheering for the Shockers on Friday night. But I hope the other Jayhawk-turned-Shocker fans got to that point with more grace than I did.

I put my left foot, then my right foot, then both feet on the coffee table to no avail.

I just couldn't take all that crowing from my buddy. He's a Wichita State University fan. Throughout the season, he kept gigging me about WSU playing the University of Kansas in basketball. I wanted him humbled, and the Shockers' loss to the Bradley Braves in the Missouri Valley Conference tournament offered the perfect opportunity. That's when I said it. That's when I went to my University of Kansas basketball bag of braggadocio.

"Why don't you worry about beating Bradley first?" I said. "Then we'll talk about you folks playing KU." Even then, he wouldn't stop: "Remember, the Shockers beat KU back in the '80s," he'd say. I told him that if you need a time machine or if you have to go back to Deuteronomy in the Old Testament to find your most recent glory days, then that's a pretty sad situation. But his good-natured ribbing was getting to me.

So imagine my horror last Friday night. KU vs. Bradley. I was in my basement, adhering to all my game-time superstitions: I had to sit on a particular end of the couch; I had to have my left foot on the table; the overhead track lighting had to be on bright, but no other lights in the basement could be on; if anyone walked into the room, I had to change the channel.

Stupid stuff, you might think, but it carried the Jayhawks to an improbable victory over the University of Oklahoma after being down by 16 with 4 minutes left. But Friday, no amount of couch contorting offered relief for my team. I put my left foot, then my right foot, then both feet on the coffee table to no avail.

Flicking the lights on and off couldn't perk up the defense or cause those three-point shots to rattle out of the rim. And when that Bradley player tossed in that flaky, lucky, off-the-backboard three-pointer at the end of the half to put the Braves up 10, I really wanted to change the channel.

Then the phone rang. It was my tormentor. I ignored his call but he caught up with me the next day and seemingly every day since then. "Beat Bradley first, huh?" he clucked. Yes, KU has had a couple of painful losses in the NCAA, I said. But we'll have a great team returning next year. And in KU's recent history—let me emphasize recent—the program made it to two Final Fours, one NCAA champion ship game and an Elite Eight loss in overtime. "But now your team is home," he shot back. "That's two years in a row, isn't it?"

What a revolting development. Do KU fans behave this way? Are we as obnoxious? Insufferable? Maybe. Either way, I'm going to change. No boorish behavior. KU is college basketball royalty, the cradle of college basketball. The progeny of James Naismith, the inventor of the game. And this year, Jayhawk fans, the Shockers are carrying the basketball banner for the state.

Those of us who love the team from Lawrence have to adjust. I, for one, am aspiring to better behavior by cheering loudly for my hometown Shockers. But not before reminding my friend that it took a KU man, Coach Mark Turgeon, to get the WSU program back into the limelight. Go Shocks!

Then the phone rang. It was my tormentor. I ignored his call but he caught up with me the next day and seemingly every day since then.

III. CLOROX 2

As an African American child, the Reverend Clay Calloway always wrestled with the notion of being washed as white as snow. "I've come to believe that the blood of Christ is more like Clorox 2—it whitens whites AND brightens colors."

IN THE IMAGE OF GOD

July 18, 2003

Before the Re-Imagining community declined from 2,200 devotees 10 years ago to 200 last month; before organizers regrettably junked plans for any future meetings and closed their Twin Cities offices; before it faded from our ecclesiastical radar screens, Re-Imagining changed the world.

At conferences assembled by so-called radical feminists, mainline Protestants and Roman Catholics celebrated feminine images and names for God, and challenged Christianity's patriarchal traditions. Pointing to scriptural references such as "the womb of God" and "God in labor with the world," they advocated calling God "Mother" as well as "Father." They summoned God's feminine aspect, "Sophia" (wisdom). They railed against oppressive male dominance in the church.

Conservative Christians accused them of idolatry and called them "fem-damentalists." Re-Imagining was a flash point for feminist theological controversies that swept the major denominations. I covered the flap and fallout as a young religion writer at *The Courier-Journal* in Louisville, Kentucky.

One black Baptist organization regularly asked women to move to the back of the room when voting took place. "How can they see the oppression of the white power structure and not see what they are doing to women in God's house?" a woman asked.

Similar issues rippled through the Southern Baptist Convention, the nation's largest Protestant denomination. The SBC agenda excluded women from pastoral roles. Inevitably, the crosshairs fixed on Molly Marshall, a tenured theology professor at its flagship institution, the Southern Baptist Theological Seminary in Louisville. On a campus where the faculty had to sign statements pledging fidelity with the belief that women should not serve as pastors,

Marshall had long taught the course preparing students for precisely that role.

A year after she received a prestigious interdenominational teaching award, conservative trustees removed Marshall, described as the most intelligent and best-educated Baptist woman of the 20th century, from the faculty. Her "failure to relate constructively" to the SBC and her "violations of seminary principles" led to the administration's actions, the president said then. I found reflections of my own religious angst in the tears of Marshall's devastated students as well as in the rhetoric of Re-Imagining. Aspects of the conferences were quite disturbing, but I realized that participants were searching for something.

I had searched for nationalist and pan-African images of God the same way Marshall and feminist theologians sought meaningful gender imagery.

I had searched for nationalist and pan-African images of God the same way Marshall and feminist theologians sought meaningful gender imagery. I learned the value of Afrocentric theology for people who had absorbed so many negative images of themselves that they simply couldn't "love their neighbors" as they loved themselves. They didn't love themselves enough.

I've also come to believe that the grace sustaining us is less like the traditional bleach that washes us "white as snow" and more like Clorox 2, which brightens colors as well as whitens whites. And though God's racial makeup shouldn't matter, since God should be worshiped in spirit and in truth, I've often wondered if such remedial concepts would even be necessary if more people embraced a more historically accurate image of Jesus.

So as the women of Re-Imagining laughed and cried and prayed their way to a greater understanding of their faith, they lifted everyone's God-consciousness as well. Great social movements benefit the collective as well as individuals. Re-Imagining helped erode social conventions that made many women feel like uninvited guests at God's table of grace. Before it faded, it illuminated—for Christian men and women—the value of an earnest quest for closeness to God.

RUNNING RIGHT WAY PAYS OFF

June 1, 2005

Three years ago, Brenda Alonzo was running. Running with the wrong crowd. Running into trouble. Running from the bright, thoughtful person she could be.

She realized that she was hurtling through life so quickly, she'd never stopped long enough to see all of the opportunities rushing by her. With all that running, she was getting nowhere fast, but one of those opportunities found her last week.

I wrote about Brenda last year in a story about one girl's struggle to put her violent past behind her. She was actually running when she was shot in December of 2002, chasing a carload of gang-bangers who drove by them on the street, jeering. She'd followed her "homies" toward the car in case they had to fight, but one of the bangers in the car drew a gun and fired. A bullet tore through her right shoulder as she turned to run.

A reputation becomes a living thing after a while, she said. Symbiotic. You live off it and it lives off you.

But if a bullet was ever a blessing, this one was. It slowed down the North High School student long enough for her to think about her life. She lay in a hospital bed, gritting her teeth and waiting for her homies to walk through that door and comfort her. To ask if she was OK. To tell her they cared that she ran into danger with them.

None of them showed up. And when she got out of the hospital, they wouldn't even stand by her, afraid that the next bullet could wind up in their shoulder. Or in their head. So she stood alone.

Brenda went from a struggling student to an honor roll student. She's been a peer mediator for other girls dealing with many of the same issues she faced. She's addressed the local school board. And this week, she was named a Dell Scholar.

Dell Scholars is a national scholarship program for AVID (Advancement Via Individual Determination) students. The winners were announced last week. Of the 161 scholarships the program awarded, only 16 went to students outside Texas and California. Kansas had two winners: Brenda and her classmate, Jessica Eichbauer. The scholarship totals $20,000 for four years.

When I met Brenda last year, she talked about her previously fearsome persona. A reputation becomes a living thing after a while, she said. Symbiotic. You live off it and it lives off you. She fed that previous persona with escalating acts of violence. It fed her the attention and so-called friendships she craved. But Brenda closed the door on that life in the hospital when none of those friends bothered to walk through that door.

New friends, however, told her that she was smart. That she was a leader. She liked that. She plans to nourish this new persona either by studying psychology at Wichita State University, or by becoming an immigration lawyer. And through it all, she never ran from any of her responsibilities as a mommy.

Today, she's running again, but in a new direction. This time, ahead of the pack instead of with a pack. This time, over barriers. This time, away from her past, and toward a bright future.

A Sense of Justice—The Lessons He Learned in His Close-knit Family Are at the Heart of Wichita Native Ron Walter's Success

September 17, 1996

Ronald Walters piloted Jesse Jackson's 1984 presidential campaign. He ran all the floor operations at the Democratic Convention in 1988. He has headed university departments much of his academic life. And in the coming months, he will address the French Senate on human rights, meet with former South African President F.W. de Klerk and make appearances as an analyst on *NewsHour with Jim Lehrer.*

It's all a long way from North Madison Street in Wichita, where Walters grew up. But wherever Walters' work takes him—across the country or around the globe—a piece of him still belongs to Wichita. And although many Wichitans may be unfamiliar with him, Walters tries to return as often as possible and keep in touch with his roots. Each visit, such as the one earlier this month to watch a play written in his honor, is special. Each visit also underlines the importance of his close-knit family in his life.

Walters' father, Gilmar Walters, was an outspoken man, one of the most prolific letters-to-the-editor writers *The Wichita Eagle* ever had. His mother, Maxine Walters, was a civil rights investigator for the Kansas Commission on Civil Rights. Many of his relatives were involved in breaking down the barriers to black achievement. An uncle was a radio man with the famous Tuskegee Airmen; some aunts picketed a local grocery store for not hiring black checkout clerks; other relatives were star athletes or scholars.

"My dad instilled in us walking with your head up," said Marcia Walters, Ron Walters' younger sister and one of his six siblings. "He (Dad) said, 'Nobody on this Earth,

As a teenage stock clerk working downtown, Ron Walters passed black people waiting in long, segregated lines during their lunch breaks.

on this Earth, should be able to make you bow your head.' Whatever Ronnie did, it was inspired by our parents."

Education was stressed at home. There were grown-up conversations at the dinner table, a house full of books and reference material, and consequences for unacceptable grades.

Robert Newby, Walters' childhood friend, said Walters was able to excel in school and still be popular. According to Newby, now a department chairman at Central Michigan University, Walters had a crooner's voice and was a pretty good dancer. "He was a person who could walk in both worlds," Newby said. "He was very popular. And he was a leader."

As a teenage stock clerk working downtown, Ron Walters passed black people waiting in long, segregated lines during their lunch breaks. "That line of black people waiting for lunch is still in my mind today," Walters said. "It is an insulting, degrading image that I saw on a daily basis."

That scene, along with preaching from his parents that he was as good as anyone else, developed in him a profound sense of what was just and what was unjust. It led to one of the most important stands he took in his life. "That's always been a part of him," Newby said. "He has always been committed to justice." Injustice was something he could not sit still for—unless of course, sitting down could change things.

In the summer of 1958, Walters organized a sit-in at the Dockum Drug Store at the southeast corner of Broadway and Douglas. At the time, he was a 20-year-old East High School graduate who was studying at Wichita State University and was president of the local NAACP's youth group. Other, similar sit-ins received much greater publicity, particularly one in Greensboro, North Carolina. But Wichita's was the first.

"I've had to keep telling people, 'Look, it's not a surprise that this happened here,' " Walters said during his visit to Wichita this month. "It is an untold story."

What may be even more surprising is that the youth

branch's sit-in, staged over four to five weeks, took place without the support of the local branch or national office of the National Association for the Advancement of Colored People. It also did not have the blessing of many parents, who kept their children home out of fear for their safety. "You hear the accounts now, and all of black Wichita was out at the drugstore," Walters said.

Walters organized the demonstration with his cousin, Carol Parks. Parks was still leading the sit-in weeks later when the drugstore owners finally succumbed to the pressure; Walters was away on National Guard duty.

Encouraged by their success, the youths took on an ice cream parlor across the street from East High School and other eating establishments around town. Barrier after barrier dropped. "That (string of events) fundamentally changed my life," Walters said. "I was emboldened. All of us were."

Standing Up In America's Heartland, a play about the Dockum sit-in, was performed by the current NAACP youth group earlier this month. "I enjoyed it," Walters said after attending the performance. "I think that the line was fairly true to what had actually happened."

Walters eventually left Wichita to attend historically black Fisk University in Nashville, Tennessee. He couldn't afford to come home often, but when he called home, everyone—his four brothers and two sisters—gathered around the phone and waited their turn. When he wrote, the letter was read aloud and there was a word or two for everyone. The family has remained close throughout Walters' life.

And what a life it has been. Take a peek at his resume: On the academic front, Walters has written three books, 85 articles and four research monographs. He has been chairman of the Afro-American studies department at Brandeis University in Waltham, Massachusetts, and chairman of the political science department at Howard University in Washington. He is now a professor of government and politics at the University of Maryland—a position he recently accepted after a great deal of courting by the school.

On the political front, he has been an invited guest of

Encouraged by their success, the youths took on an ice cream parlor across the street from East High School and other eating establishments around town.

the World Conference on Sanctions Against South Africa and a member of President Clinton's delegation charged with monitoring the recent South African elections. He has been a member of the US Symposium Delegation to the 2nd Festival of African Art and Culture in Lagos, Nigeria. And he has been a guest of the deputy prime minister of Jamaica.

And there's a lot, lot more—both academically and politically. James Turner, director of the Africana Studies and Research Center at Cornell University in Ithaca, New York, said Walters' work is highly respected in academic circles and often influences national public policy.

Marcia Walters said she cried when it was her turn—well, she cried on everyone's turn, she said.

But Turner said Walters, who is in his late 50s, rarely seeks the limelight. "His name rarely appears up front," Turner said. "When people want to get things done, they don't call Cornel West, they don't call Skip (Henry Louis) Gates—not to take anything from them—they call Ron Walters," Turner said. "They know he's not the showy kind. He's going to do all of the work."

Turner called Walters the living personification of academic excellence and social responsibility. "There are very few people I respect as much as Ron Walters," Turner said. "All of us love and respect him, and we say that unashamedly."

If Walters seems almost too perfect, it is worthwhile to let his younger brother Gerald flesh the picture out a bit with childhood stories. Gerald remembers a time when he and Ron were playing catch near the house. "Ron kept tossing a baseball higher and higher over my head until I couldn't reach it," Gerald Walters said, "and it broke out a window." When their father came out, "Ron said it was my fault," Gerald Walters recalled, smiling. "And they believed him because, 'Ron wouldn't do anything like that.' "

There was another time when their father brought home a truck-load of dirt that needed to be spread on the lawn. After spreading dirt for a few minutes, Gerald recalled, Ron said to his father: "I have an important paper that I need to get out. Can I go up to the university (Wichita State) and do some research?" His father waved him off to do the research.

A couple of hours later, Gerald did the same thing, and headed over to the campus activity center. There, he found his older brother, leaning over a pool table. "He just smiled at me when I walked in," Gerald Walters said.

These days, Ron Walters still has a great sense of humor. There is nothing really subtle or dry about it; he simply likes to laugh.

But as deft as he may be in the worlds of politics and world affairs, expressions of love for his family can arrest him emotionally. At his 30th wedding anniversary a few years ago, Walters and his wife Pat decided to renew their wedding vows in the African tradition. There was an elaborate ceremony and a moment when each of them would talk about what they meant to each other. Walters couldn't do it. "He just broke down," his sister Marcia Walters said. "He just grabbed her and hugged her and told her he loved her. He didn't get much further than that."

And in August, he was back in Wichita for his mother's 75th birthday party. Walters' father passed away in 1989. At the party, everyone stood and said something about the family's matriarch. Marcia Walters said she cried when it was her turn—well, she cried on everyone's turn, she said.

Marcia Walters recalled that when it was Ron's turn, he said, "Mother, I love you, and Mother. . .I. . .and. . .you know. . ." Ron moved his hands in circles, searching for the right words. Finally, overcome with the moment, he said, "You know I can't do this." "He just hugged her and said he loved her. He's got a soft heart."

CIVIL RIGHTS GIANT TO SPEAK IN WICHITA—DIANE NASH SOUGHT RACIAL EQUALITY IN THE '60S THROUGH NONVIOLENT ACTIVISM

April 4, 2002

When a terrorist bomb ripped through a Birmingham, Alabama, Sunday school class and killed four little girls in September 1963, Diane Nash's heart crumbled. Her faith in nonviolent social change buckled, too. As an activist, she'd risked her life for that cause. Violence, she thought, should never have the last word in a civilized society.

But in the middle of a voter registration campaign, she and her husband found themselves darkly wondering if the monsters who did this should be hunted down and killed. "We wouldn't be able to respect ourselves if we did nothing about it," recalled Nash recently from her Chicago home. "One of the things we considered was making sure that whoever did it, died."

It was one episode from a dynamic life of activism Nash will bring with her to Wichita on Saturday. She is the keynote speaker at a Friends University-sponsored conference on the legacy of the 1960s. Conference organizer Gretchen Eick said Nash is considered a civil rights giant in the books *The Children,* by David Halberstam, and *Freedom's Daughters,* by Lynne Olson. "She has a kind of idealism that is important for us to recapture, a real mantra that is very relevant to today," said Eick, associate professor of history at Friends.

University of Maryland professor Ron Walters, a Wichita native and Nash's classmate at Fisk University in Nashville, remembered her as strong-willed, exceedingly pleasant and deeply devoted to the cause. "I know that she will have an interesting story to tell," he said. She does.

Today, she pays the bills working in real estate. She

also takes occasional speaking engagements and is writing a book about her life. Born in 1938, she grew up a teen beauty queen in a Chicago home that consciously suppressed talk of racial identity, despite glancing but painful Northern discrimination. After enrolling at Fisk, however, she found herself in the racially-obsessed South, challenging a different, scalding brand of segregation. She shunned leadership roles, but classmates quickly noticed her dedication. Before she knew it, she was reluctantly leading a swelling social movement.

As a student, she once ambushed then-Nashville Mayor Ben West, getting him to admit at a press conference that he didn't personally agree with discrimination. Her poised and persistent questions, and his honest, albeit coerced answers, opened lunch counters there. Books describe her as a beautiful woman confidently walking the front lines of one of the ugliest chapters of American history. Nash said she may have appeared outwardly defiant, but she was inwardly terrified. She'd sit in class, she said, palms on her desk as if to steady herself, as the clock chipped away at the time leading to the next demonstration.

Nash said she may have appeared outwardly defiant, but she was inwardly terrified.

Her fears drowned out the instructor's voice: What if someone following me gets hurt? What if they find out how afraid I am? What if we're beaten to death? By the time class ended, she'd left palm prints of sweat on the wooden desktop. "I was always so scared," she said. "But the movement had a way of allowing me and others to discover things inside ourselves that we didn't even know were there."

Some things, though, were harder to find. Her devotion to nonviolence developed slowly. She once wondered why she'd wasted her time in classes where activists recreated the shouting and shoving demonstrators typically faced at lunch counters. But after seeing nonviolent resistance in practice, its potential as a weapon for change crystallized for her.

Ultimately, nonviolence proved the right choice, she said, but she was tantalizingly close to choosing rage after the Birmingham Sunday school bombing.

She and the Rev. James Bevel, whom she later divorced, eventually decided that people could protect their children if they got the right to vote. They promised themselves, God and each other that they would help make that happen. They led voter registration campaigns and organized legions of "Freedom Riders"—student volunteers bused in from the North—who staffed them.

Their work, she said, paid off. "As horrible as that crime was, the thing that would have been even worse would be that their deaths would be unanswered, that nothing happened. The fact that the right to vote was a direct result of their deaths somehow helps. We'd kept our promise."

LOST IN LOVE AND LOVING MUSIC, PAIR ENDURES

November 28, 2004

Every Wednesday night at Chelsea's Bar and Grill, people show up to hear good music—and to see the love story. The dinner crowd sits scattered around the dimly lit room sipping Chardonnay and slicing away on prime rib. The wait staff navigates the maze of tables smiling and patting shoulders.

Then, a dignified older couple, Maxine Therese Gunheim and her husband, Myran Winfield Gunheim, appear in the hallway. Maxine glides along in a black sequin blouse, her white hair flipped at her shoulders. Myran, in a dark suit and tie, gently leads her through the room, holding her arm with one hand and carrying her purse in the other.

About six years ago, she began to lose her eyesight.

They arrive at the hard-polished piano in the corner. He helps her take her seat on the bench and sits down beside her. Then she begins to play. Beautifully. "On the Street Where You Live." "Strangers in the Night." Other stand-bys.

Everyone watches. And smiles. One couple shows up almost weekly. The first time they saw Maxine, they tipped her $100. People show up sometimes just to see Maxine and Myran, says Angela Kuhn, who's worked at Chelsea's for two years. Spectators are always full of questions: "How old is she?" "How long have they been married?" "Is she blind?" "I thought they were just precious," Kuhn said of the first time she saw the couple. "I think it is so wonderful to think that people could stay married for so long."

Maxine has played at Chelsea's for five years, says general manager Jason Fisher. Before that, she routinely visited Piccadilly West for the Sunday brunch, occasionally playing the piano. "They were such a dear couple," said Fisher, who eventually hired her. "They really touch the customers."

Maxine grew up in a home filled with music. Her mother sang everything from church music to opera; her father was a concert pianist. But like many fathers, he didn't much care for his daughter's first love. He considered music a tough business for men and impossible for women. Eventually, even he had to realize that this love wouldn't wait. And it didn't.

Maxine wrote children's musicals such as *The Snow-pudding Princess*, wrote her own piano sheet music, and played to audiences all over the country. About six years ago, she began to lose her eyesight and, with it, her music.

That's when Myran, her husband of 27 years, stepped in. They'd sit on the bench together in front of the piano and he helped her feel her way through the darkness. What had once been at her fingertips now seemed miles away. When she said she couldn't, he'd tell her she could. And then he'd select another song.

"I was so humbled," Maxine said of losing her sight, "but my husband was very calm and supportive." It took awhile, but with God's grace and Myran's help, the music came back. Now Maxine plays almost every day. At Chelsea's. At Kwan Court. At the Museum of World Treasures. At the Wichita Art Museum. At Botanica. Wherever she can. Whenever she can.

At each place, people come to see her play. They see her attentive husband sitting beside her, and they smile. And little do they know that the love story on display isn't just about the sweet little couple in front of them. It's also about the woman on the keys, lost in her music, lost in the performance, lost in love.

SANDERS BLINDSIDED—GIFT FROM TEACHER IGNITED POWERFUL MEMORIES

January 23, 2004

Waiting in the back of a long line at North High School last weekend, many people worried if Barry Sanders, scheduled to autograph books from 2:30 to 4:30 p.m., would pull his early retirement act again. But he hung in, scribbling in the last book sometime after 9.

Barry had shown up in a giving mood that day but would receive a gift he never saw coming. The event—complete with honor guard, spirit squads and one heck of a marching band—had been planned around the life of one special person, Barry's older sister Nancy.

Nancy Sanders, to whom he dedicated his best-selling book, *Barry Sanders: Now You See Him . . .* , died in 1991 at the age of 27 from the autoimmune disease scleroderma.

Proceeds from the day's book sales and donations benefited scleroderma research. Barry surpassed his goal of raising $10,000 (he has raised $14,500 as of Wednesday) and gave hundreds of people warm memories on a cold day.

But there was someone else there also in a giving mood. After about four hours, a man in line unceremoniously presented Barry with a worn sheet of paper. The man said the paper was a worksheet of Nancy's he'd saved from her time as his student in the early 1970s. Barry, who's as composed as Kansas City Chiefs' Coach Dick Vermeil is weepy, looked up, clearly moved. No sooner than Barry had said thank you, the man had dissolved into the waiting crowd.

Hours later at Barry's parents' house, Barry, his sister Donna and their mother, Shirley, poured over the sheet, touched by the gesture and amazed that someone would have saved the paper for all these years. It listed, in Nancy's small, neat handwriting, her name, her parents' names and jobs, and her siblings, oldest to youngest.

Donna guessed that the man who'd delivered it must have been Val Cheatham. He taught gifted students at OK Elementary School, which the Sanders kids and I had attended. Curious, I looked him up.

Mr. Cheatham (that's what I've always called him) explained that he'd long kept scrapbooks of his students. It began, he said, when he once split his pants doing calisthenics with some students. At the end of the year, one of the students sent him a patch with a clever little note attached and his memory library was born.

It was as if we'd found a tangible piece of the person who'd left us 12 years ago.

The books make for great reference material when former students write to reminisce. "I can look back and tell them little things about their hobbies and who they were in class with," he said, smiling through the phone. "They think I have a great memory."

He remembered Nancy, and when he learned Barry would be in town, he retrieved the book of Nancy's mementos. He found the sheet he gave to Barry among group photos and scenes from plays she'd performed in.

Mr. Cheatham, now retired, said he asked students to fill out the sheets because he was interested in how family size and birth order impacted personality. Nancy, he said, was soft-spoken and aware of things beyond her age and knowledge, and she wrote stories rich with personal detail. She was a bright, thoughtful child.

As amazing as it was that Mr. Cheatham had saved that paper was the paper's impact on all of us who knew Nancy. It was as if we'd found a tangible piece of the person who'd left us 12 years ago. It was an example of how nice it can be to find memories of lost loved ones still shining in the hearts and minds of people around us. And how seemingly meaningless items can ignite powerful memories.

DON'T MISTAKE BARRY'S RESERVE AS NOT CARING

August 8, 2004

[Note: This was filed from Barry's Hall of Fame induction ceremony in Canton, Ohio. Mark McCormick has been friends with Barry Sanders since kindergarten. He helped write the autobiography *Barry Sanders: Now You See Him.*]

I can remember the outfit Barry Sanders wore for his prom-king photo at North High. The jacket kind of bunched in the armpits. The pants were a little tight. The pant legs were so high that they would have been bone-dry in six inches of water. It didn't fit him very well. Neither has fame.

Many of fame's aspects just seem to chafe him. He famously avoids interviews. Some of the questions from media may have been too intimate, as though they were riding up. He's made relatively few public appearances. Heck, the day Wichita celebrated his winning the Heisman Trophy—a day filled with cheers, rallies and proclamations—he borrowed an old trench coat from me to avoid being noticed.

In the past few months, he even put off meeting with the world-renowned artist sculpting his Hall of Fame bust. The other enshrinees sat for the artist in February at the Pro Bowl. The sculptor gathered measurements and took photos. But Barry skipped the Pro Bowl. And with the drop-dead date for the sitting looming on a Thursday, Barry was still negotiating a Wednesday sitting.

With his reaction to the sculpture, and his M.O. (modus operandi) when it comes to parades, interviews, luncheons, dinners, ceremonies, receptions and halftime shows, you get the sense that Barry would be satisfied with a registered letter and certificate notifying him that he'd been inducted and a coupon for a free smoothie.

We shouldn't make the mistake of thinking he doesn't care, though the Kansan in him cries out, "Why all the fuss?" Barry said Friday in Canton, "I couldn't wait to get here. I can't wait to put on that jacket and share the time with family and friends. It's a special time."

Hall of Fame defensive lineman Deacon Jones said he and the other former inductees are placing bets as to whether Barry cries today during his induction.

Back in 1997, I thought Barry might be dreading the prospect of breaking the 2,000-yard single-season rushing mark. As that incredible mirage morphed into a possibility—only two other men had reached the 2,000-yard mark in a season—I just knew that he was hating all of the attention that his talent had focused on him.

But at dinner in Detroit the night before the game, Barry was happier than I'd seen him in years. He was excited about the game, seemingly energized by the long odds. That's when it clicked for me that the challenge of it all, the test, the curiosity of whether or not he could do it, is what drove him. Not the attention.

That's when it clicked for me that the challenge of it all, the test, the curiosity of whether or not he could do it, is what drove him.

These challenges drove him all the way to Canton, where today, Barry's father, William, will give a rousing introduction for his son.

The crowd at Fawcett Stadium—filled with admiring former players and faithful fans—will cheer loudly for the man for whom the spotlight was something to flee rather than something to demand that your agent secure for you. The ill-fitting suit of fame may make him a little uncomfortable. But I'll tell you what: Hordes of proud Wichitans and Kansans and Oklahomans who followed his career think it suits him just fine. The man who ran like the Devil, but prayed to God, the man who embarrassed defenders with ankle breaking moves but who never felt the need to show anyone up with a cell phone in the end zone, suits us just fine.

I hope he understands that when people nominate you for something, whether it's for prom king or for the Hall, it's usually not for you. It's for what you gave them, whether it's memories, inspiration, or a feeling of pride. And that effort put into carving the bust and shuttling him from interview to interview and clapping for him at dinners isn't meant to embarrass him.

It's for all the people who are proud of him. Folks who will miss all of the heart palpitations he caused every Sunday when he got the ball. People who are thankful that he sat still long enough so that everyone could tell him that. That's why today is so fitting: His Hall of Fame coat, like his career, was tailor made.

COURTING FAITH: ABOUT 400 AREA YOUTHS GET FREE TIPS FROM SOME TOP ATHLETES AS WELL AS A MESSAGE OF SALVATION

September 14, 1997

A Christian's decision to accept Jesus Christ into his or her life is deeply personal, but is often expressed in a very public way—usually by a long walk from a pew to the front of the church.

Shaina Stanton found herself in a similar circumstance Saturday near the end of a sports clinic at Wichita State University's Heskett Center. She eventually made the walk—from her seat in the bleachers, not a pew—but needed Brandon Reed, and his memories of his grandmother, to help her take the first step.

Shaina, 9, and Brandon, 11, were just two of the roughly 400 students who came to the clinic for a few hours of athletic instruction and a Gospel message organizers hoped would last a lifetime. The free sports clinic was one of several events leading up to the Oct. 26-29 Heartland Festival '97 with Franklin Graham at the Kansas Coliseum. More than 15,000 people are expected nightly during the four nights of praying, singing and preaching.

Saturday, after a morning of instruction in baseball, basketball, volleyball and soccer, the students—Shaina and Brandon among them—piled onto bleachers to listen to a message from ex-NBA star, Bobby Jones. Jones, the defensive stopper who could flash to the hoop with either his right or his left hand, said there was a time in his spiritual life when he didn't know which way to turn.

"I was not happy at all with my life," Jones told the group, "I didn't have an answer to what to live for in my life." Jones explained how he wrestled with his ego, pride,

104

and stubbornness before turning his life over to Christ. He asked the youths to do the same. "God has plans for you," Jones said. "He'll guide your life."

Shaina wanted to come forward, but the distance from her seat in the bleachers to the floor where Jones was speaking seemed a million miles away. Shaina's mother, Jackie, recalled, "She said, 'Mom, I've made a decision, but I don't want to go down there.' " Jones extended his arm, encouraging the students to come forward. For a brief moment, no one moved. But then Brandon, sitting in what seemed to be the last row of bleachers, came bounding down to the floor.

Suddenly, a horde of other youths followed, Shaina included. "I was just kind of scared to come down," Shaina said afterwards, grinning. "I just wanted to make sure I was a Christian." Brandon said his grandmother, who died a few years ago, wanted to make sure he was a Christian. When he visited her, she took him to church, encouraged him to pray and helped him read the Bible. "She was a strong Christian," Brandon said. Asked if he thought he was a leader, what with everyone following him down the bleachers and all, Brandon smiled and said, "I guess I just want to be a Christian and to go to Heaven."

Tim Robertson, state director for the Fellowship of Christian Athletes and coordinator for the event, said the clinic sought to give children "a picture of what we feel is important—a relationship with Jesus Christ." The clinic drew the youth in with the likes of Jones, ex-New York Yankee and Mickey Mantle teammate Bobby Richardson, and the first American to play professional soccer in Brazil, Desmond Armstrong.

The influence of sports on American youth is incredible, Robertson said. It is apparent in the heavily swooshed shirts, shorts and shoes the children were wearing, and the focused attention they gave to the athletes instructing them, he said. Robertson said whether coaches and athletes want to be or not, they are role models. And apparently for Shaina and Brandon, so are peers and grandmothers.

Shaina wanted to come forward, but the distance from her seat in the bleachers to the floor where Jones was speaking seemed a million miles away.

THOUGHTS OF DAD INSPIRE A SON'S GRATITUDE

June 18, 2006

I can remember crawling under my dad's trench coat and holding onto his leg after he and my mother separated. And, later, I remember spending evenings sitting on the porch, a little suitcase under my arm, watching the end of the block for his long Cadillac to round the comer and scoop me up for the weekend.

I followed him everywhere, and in the days before enlightened child safety, I stood on the seat next to him

My father, Joseph Langston McCormick, Jr.
Courtesy Mark McCormick.

with my arm around his neck as he drove. I hated that I wasn't named after him, Joseph Langston McCormick, but relished every instance when someone called me "Little Joe."

I never strayed far from his lap. Everywhere we went, I can remember people saying, "That boy sho' loves his daddy." It has forever been thus. From the time I was old enough to dial a phone, I called him collect wherever he was living—Los Angeles, Oklahoma City, Denver, New Orleans.

I used to burrow through his leather shaving bag and count the Joe Camel coupons in there. I'd open his black metal lunch box to see what he'd had for lunch that day. I'd park the front wheels of my kid-size plastic car on the stairs and crawl under it, imitating the weekend hours Daddy spent tinkering on cars in our backyard.

I wrecked several of his real cars before I was 5, driving them off jacks or backing them into other cars he'd parked in front of the house. (Don't blame my parents. I was just a bad kid.) Instead of being angry, he'd laugh and brag about how I said I was "wheeling" when he and my frantic mother pulled me out of the wreckage unharmed.

I seemed to be his greatest source of laughs. When I "caught" my first fish, about as long as my finger, he said, I made my grandmother get out of bed to clean it and cook it for me. To be honest, I don't remember catching the fish. He caught it but said I did to make me feel good.

Once when I saw him skinning a squirrel he'd knocked out of a tree, he said, I wandered up and asked him, "Daddy, why are you taking his clothes off?" And when I shot a rabbit with my pellet gun, only to have the pellet bounce off, I threw the pellet gun down in frustration and Daddy roared with laughter. So much of who I am is a reflection of him. My sense for the importance of family history comes from his stories about how my grandfather was one of 29 kids.

He talks about a chicken named Lazarus who lived 30 days after having his head chopped off.

My empathy with the struggle of machinists and unions comes because he was a union boss at an aircraft plant here. And certainly, my love for a good story comes from him. He has more stories than Mother Goose, and some of them are about as believable. He talks about a chicken named Lazarus who lived 30 days after having his head chopped off. About a man with a freak enzyme in his stomach that allowed him to eat piles of food. About driving off a snow-packed road near Reno, Nevada, and surviving in a freezing ravine for three days on onions he had in the trunk.

My daddy has always been the toughest, funniest and coolest man I know. He's so much of what I'm not but wish I was: comfortable in crowds, never meeting a stranger, the center of any party. All the stand-up men I admired growing up, from my adult cousin Don Holloway to our neighbor Andrew Morrow, seemed to admire him, too.

Every boy ought to feel about his dad the way I do about mine. I laugh to myself sometimes at how little our relationship has changed across the decades. I still follow him around when I visit. I still call him almost daily. I still hang on every word of his stories, even the ones I've heard over and over. I still wish my name was Joe. And as always, this boy still loves his Daddy.

LIKE SCHOOL, MOM MARKS HER 75TH

October 2, 2005

While former students pour into North High this weekend to celebrate the school's 75th anniversary, they'll likely pause at the senior class photographs hanging in the halls. When I attended the school, I'd flip through the classes and find my mother's photo. Ethel Daniels. Class of 1945. She has always been beautiful to me, but this photo was extraordinary. I don't think I had ever seen her as happy as she seemed in that photo. Sometimes, I'd wonder where her locker had been. If she ate lunch under one of those trees on the east lawn. I'd try to imagine her walking the hallways.

Earlier this year, my sister and I found ourselves waiting for our mother in another hallway —a long one heading into the cardiac intensive care unit at Via Christi-St. Francis. After two weeks of tests, suspicion turned to possible blockages and poor valve closure in her heart. Mom's cardiologist, Thomas Ashcom, emerged after a while to say that he'd opened two blockages but couldn't navigate a coil of artery hiding a third. While he tried, my mother's heart stopped and she stopped breathing. He asked if he could place her on a ventilator temporarily.

I voted no at first. My mother has always said that she wouldn't want a machine to artificially sustain her life, and I didn't want to find myself in the position of having to take her off of it. But Dr. Ashcom said she wouldn't make it otherwise, and that she just needed a little help breathing. So, staring death in the eye, I blinked.

I rationalized that it would only be for a few minutes, but the next morning, she was still on the machine, fading. Here lay this beautiful person who had never once failed me. And the only thing she had ever asked me to do, I screwed up. She had always made me promise never to leave her on a machine, and yet, here she was.

Nurses set the ventilator at 8, which meant the machine breathed for her eight times a minute. They explained that if she began to breathe on her own, the number would rise. For two and a half days, the reading hovered at 8. Her heart valves were shot. She was too weak for the procedure to repair them. Her doctors, including Diana Crook (whom I adore), began preparing us for the worst.

Mom's high school photo kept coming to mind, and I'd run to the chapel to cry, pray and think. I'd think about how people dissolve into paper when they die—insurance policies, titles, deeds and, yes, pictures. We had already started pulling Mom's papers together.

Pretty soon, I started thinking, this precious photograph might be all that I'd have left of her. But as family arrived to say goodbye, her ventilator number jumped to 12, then to 14. Nurses and doctors cautioned us not to put too much stock in that. A day later, though, she opened her eyes. That she's at home now reading this is the most generous blessing ever. That photo is, too. I've made copies. Lots of them. I keep one on my desk here at work and one in my home office.

As I look at it now, I find it fitting that both North and my mother are celebrating 75 years. All of this happened during her 75th birthday in January. I'll never see that photo without thinking of her and that wonderful old school. I'll celebrate quietly every time I'm able to call my mother and hear her say on the other end, "Well, hello, young man!" It's a celebration I mark not only in years, but also in days.

RELIGION NOT RIDICULOUS TO BELIEVERS

October 1, 2008

If not for *Real Time,* the weekly hour of political insight and satire featuring comedian Bill Maher on Friday nights, I wouldn't have HBO. I've become quite a fan.

Except when Maher attacks religion. Sitting through his rants every week, I feel guilty about watching. Maher often calls religion a collection of fairy tales. He mocks people who believe in angels and demons. He's fond of referencing the Garden of Eden's "talking snake." Those are just taunts, but his underlying point is that religion has been dangerous, even deadly.

On Friday, Maher will release *Religulous,* a documentary billed as an "uproarious nonfiction film about the greatest fiction ever told." *Religulous,* I'm guessing, is derived from the word ridiculous, and the greatest fiction ever told intends to tweak *The Greatest Story Ever Told,* a reference to the story of Jesus.

But last week, I saw how powerfully religion moves in my own life, and how powerfully it moves through the lives of people I know and people I don't know. I offer these observations not to disprove the premise of Maher's movie, but to balance it.

You may have noticed that my column hasn't run for the past week or so. That's because I was sitting beside my mother's bed at Via Christi-St. Francis hospital, where her doctor, Thomas Ashcom, and his physician assistant, Christine Johnson, treated her for congestive heart failure.

Hospitals began as charities, as ministries even, and that was evident at Via Christi. Nurses came in and tucked her into oven-warmed blankets when she was cold. They patted her hand and called her "sweetie." And while no one mentioned God, their care and concern certainly seemed inspired by Him.

The dignity and generosity that characterized his life flowed from his faith.

During that same week, my mother's neighbor, a dear man named Andrew Morrow, died after a terrible fall and subsequent heart attack. Mr. Morrow was the greatest, most helpful neighbor ever. He was also a decorated World War II veteran who'd earned a Bronze Star. Mr. Morrow accepted Christ as his savior at 16 and was often sitting in front of the church Sunday mornings when his pastor, the Rev. Keith Cullors, arrived to open the doors. The dignity and generosity that characterized his life flowed from his faith.

During our procession to Lakeview Gardens Cemetery, I felt certain that some if not many of the people who pulled to the side of the road as we passed were doing what I do when a funeral procession passes: pray silently that God wrap those who are grieving in his arms and whisper in their ears that everything will be all right.

That's the spirit of care, concern and charity Maher misses while he focuses on religious people's imperfections. And there are imperfections. Some want to substitute belief for science. Some seem to want to impose their beliefs on other people. Some seem strangely intolerant.

But what about all the people eating today at the Lord's Diner? All of the people getting clothing from Open Door? All of the people getting homes from Mennonite Housing? All the people who'll have a place to sleep tonight because religious people have opened shelters for them? The people praying for the comfort of people they don't know?

Maher, whom I think of as brilliant, mistakenly applies logic to religion. Strange, since the love of Christ actually defies logic. Maher's application of logic to the spiritual feels every bit as pointless as applying religion to the logical—his criticism of the way many religious people apply faith to scientific issues like evolution. He's also smacking an ideology for the way some of its adherents practice it.

I'll likely go see the movie. I'm not afraid that anything he says could make me doubt my own beliefs. And the observations I'll make won't have anything to do with disproving the premise of Maher's movie. I don't have to. I see the truth of what I believe every day.

IV. Suffer the Little Children

"Jesus said: Suffer the little children to come unto me and forbid them not, for of such is the kingdom of God. Verily I say unto you, Whosoever shall not receive the kingdom of God as a little child, he shall not enter therein. And he took them up in his arms, put his hands upon them, and blessed them."

— Mark 10:14-16 King James Version

LET'S NOT RELY ON KIDS TO CATCH PREDATORS

June 21, 2006

We require children—children who aren't even old enough to consent to sex—to lead the rape prosecutions of the men who raped them. It's true. When teen and pre-teen girls have illegal sexual relations with men, parents can't rely on authorities to stop it—or to take it to court.

Such criminal cases hang on the word of children because the accused have the constitutional right to confront and cross-examine their accusers. So the child victims have to go to court and face the person they think they love, or the person they say they fear, to make a prosecution possible.

Does any of this seem backwards to anyone besides me? On one hand, we say such a child can't make a decision about her own sexuality. On the other, we allow her to frustrate or stop the prosecution of a sex offender?

I need an adult to take control at some point in the prosecutorial process. To take the steering wheel away from children already making poor choices. To grab these so-called men by the throat and squeeze. Otherwise, these snakes can go on to prey on someone else's 12-year-old.

District Attorney Nola Foulston said many underage girls refuse to testify against their boyfriends. "You may end a case that way," Foulston said, "but you sure don't start a case that way. You can't start a case with a combative, recalcitrant witness." One Wichita father says he has experienced this first hand. I'm not naming him because naming him would identify his daughter, and *The Eagle* doesn't name people who may be victims of sexual assault.

His daughter began a sexual relationship with a 19-year-old man when she was 12. She eventually told investigators that she'd had sex with the man, the father said. She gave a detailed description of the 19-year-old's body. She even

Last week, he and his wife watched in horror as news of 14-year-old Chelsea Brooks' disappearance and death unfolded.

described the motel room where the 19-year-old regularly took her to have sex, sometimes when she was supposed to be at school.

Her parents said they gave police the make, model and license plate number of his car. They gave police his address, his home phone and his cell phone number. They had letters the man had written their daughter. Still, the father said, law officials declined to pursue the case because his daughter had been uncooperative and had offered conflicting stories. So this awful relationship continued, as did the father's dogged search for help.

He said he called the district attorney's office. He said he called the Kansas Department of Social and Rehabilitation Services. None of the agencies helped him, he said. Each agency declined to comment on his claims. After repeated visits to these and other agencies yielded nothing, after the daughter defiantly continued the relationship, the father admitted beating his daughter with a belt.

His daughter was removed from the home temporarily, he said, in part because of that episode. "I understand what child abuse is," the man said. "But if I had to choose between spanking my daughter and her getting pregnant, her getting a disease she can't get rid of or, heaven forbid, her getting killed like this other 14-year-old, I will choose spanking."

Last week, he and his wife watched in horror as news of 14-year-old Chelsea Brooks' disappearance and death unfolded. They, too, had filed a protection-from-abuse order with the court, just as the Brooks' had. I understand that people have constitutional rights, but a situation that puts kids in charge is just wrong. We shouldn't be depending on children to stop these men. If ever there was a legitimate reason to amend the constitution, this would be one. A child shouldn't have say-so over prosecution when she doesn't even have say-so over her own body.

DISTURBING BEHAVIOR ON A
SCHOOL BUS*

November 5, 2006

Almost no one believed the 8-year-old girl when she said a
man on her Wichita school bus unfastened his pants, urinat-
ed into a cup and poured it out the window of the moving
bus. Even her mother was unsure, until her daughter described in detail what she saw and an on-board camera confirmed the October 25 incident.

Beyond not wanting her 8-year-old exposed to something like that, this girl's mother worries about the hint of
secrecy surrounding the incident. And so do I.

First, the man on the bus told the child not to say anything, and terrible things tend to follow the words, "Don't
tell." Second, although officials at the bus company and the
school district reported the incident to police and readily
admitted to me what had happened, no one volunteered this
information to the public until I asked. Lastly, the public
has no access to the disciplinary records of the adults en-
trusted to drive and care for students on buses.

The man on the bus, whom Durham School Services
Inc. called an attendant, not a driver, no longer works at the
company. Jim Price, general manager for Durham, could
recall no similar incident in the past. "This is an isolated
incident," he said.

I don't doubt that it is, but we have to take his word
on this. When I asked how many people had been fired or
disciplined in the past year, he said that information was
private. He's right. Durham is a private company.

He said the company conducts extensive background
checks, including searches for arrests, convictions and Department of Motor Vehicle records. It reminds employees
continually of conduct and safety issues.

"We have 500 drivers, we transport 20,000 students to
school every day," Price said. "Still, you're bound to have

If a private company is doing public work, it ought to get the same scrutiny and have the same transparency as a public entity, especially where children are concerned.

117

people who make poor judgments. We take our responsibility seriously to provide transportation for students so they can arrive safely, on time, and ready to learn every day. When we find an instance where someone is using poor judgment, we deal with it appropriately."

Susan Arensman, a spokeswoman for the Wichita school district, said the bus company responds quickly to district concerns. "Sometimes, they don't even wait for us to ask them to investigate, they do it on their own." Arensman said the district considers this incident resolved.

"To publicly announce the incident would, in essence, identify the Durham employee," she said. "There was no threat to the safety of students and only one student reported seeing what happened, to our knowledge. This was a personnel matter that was quickly investigated and dealt with immediately and appropriately."

I suspect Price and the district are on top of things. The mother said the principal performed heroically, believing the child when virtually no one else did. But we shouldn't have to take their word for it. If a private company is doing public work, it ought to get the same scrutiny and have the same transparency as a public entity, especially where children are concerned.

Although there was no sexual intent in this incident, a child was exposed to what amounted to a flashing. Worse, had you not been reading *The Eagle* this morning, you likely would never have known about it.

I'm not comfortable with that, and you shouldn't be, either.

'Cover Up!' And Pass the Tweezers

May 28, 2006

OK, I'm officially an old fart.

Not because I feel old (it's not the years, it's the miles). Not because I'm less and less able to relate to or participate in the latest fads. And not because I'm graying faster than South Florida. I'm an old fart because seeing teenage girls in skimpy outfits holding up car wash signs at intersections finally has gotten under my skin. I don't know how it happened, or when it happened, but now, I'm a prude.

All I know is that when I pulled up at an intersection in east Wichita last weekend and saw a bunch of teenage girls jumping up and down in almost nothing, I caught myself whispering, "Young ladies, please go and cover yourselves!"

Then I thought to myself, "Gee, that's one of the primary criterion of old-fartdom, that and bushy eyebrows and ear hair." But that's exactly where I am. I can't figure out if I'm just behind the times or if behinds are supposed to be all up in my face nowadays.

All of this has kind of crept up on me. Little by little over the years, jeans have crept downward on young bodies to where they are now, slung low on the hips. Small-of-the-back tattoos make regular appearances in public places like restaurants, as do tiny tops.

I feel like someone on the council of elders from the movie Footloose. Next I'll be preaching against makeup and dancing. But I can't help how I feel. I don't have a daughter, but I have nieces. And frankly, no matter how worthy the fundraising cause, the thought of them dancing around a busy intersection with barely anything on leaves me blushing.

They shouldn't have to wear full-body outfits, with the long underwear, the knee-high dress over that and the poofy

I also realize that my crankiness toward these young ladies may be tinged with some male hypocrisy.

hat and parasol. But I wish there were a middle ground instead of so much mid-section. That's not a commentary on the young women at these intersections innocently raising money for their particular cause. But in a society where kids are already sexualized early and are exposed to far too much, I don't want to let this lie as harmless.

And I'm not just cranky about these teenyboppers, I'm cranky in general about so many people out begging for donations. Pull up to a stoplight, and someone with a big bucket with the word "children" written across it comes shaking it at your car window. You're walking out of some big-box department store and someone has a table set up to accost you just outside the exit.

I also realize that my crankiness toward these young ladies may be tinged with some male hypocrisy. Men whoop and claw at professional cheerleaders and exotic dancers, but become Puritans when a daughter or niece exposes too much ankle. So maybe it is just me making more than warranted out of the less these young ladies were wearing.

Maybe I just have to accept my new identity as a curmudgeon. I came by it honestly. I used to hear old ladies telling young girls who wore tight or skimpy clothing to "Go cover your shame," and I can remember my aunt's shock at my sister's sporting of a miniskirt.

My dad once told me a speech should be like a woman's skirt: long enough to cover the subject but short enough to be interesting. I used to think all of that stuff was funny. Not anymore. So, it's official. I'm an old fart.

Now if you'll please excuse me, I have some eyebrows and ear hair to tweeze.

TEEN DATING VIOLENCE IS FAR TOO COMMON

April 17, 2005

You may not remember Raeshawnda Wheaton, but you should, particularly if you have a daughter with a boyfriend. Her life came to a horrific end after she got caught up in a bruising cycle of teen dating violence that too many girls too readily accept as normal.

Later this year, we'll mark the fifth anniversary of the day Wichita police found 18-year-old Raeshawnda's body in the bedroom of her duplex on North Erie. She'd been shot to death. They found her sitting with her back against a wall, clutching a pillow as if to shield herself.

A couple of weeks before, Raeshawnda's boyfriend beat her ferociously. He blackened her eye and injured her jaw. Her friends had to grind up her Thanksgiving dinner so she could eat it. Months before, he'd stuck a gun in her face.

I thought of her this week when I heard that police had arrested 18-year- old Aaron Stricker for allegedly punching his 17-year-old girlfriend in the face, breaking her nose and cracking her eye socket. Prosecutors charged Stricker with a level four aggravated battery, the highest charge possible. His preliminary hearing is set for April 19.

I cringe at the thought of how many girls this must happen to every day without our noticing. Lt. Tom Bridges, commander of the Wichita Police Department's sex crimes and domestic violence investigative unit, said it's difficult to discern whether teen dating violence is increasing. Police fold incidents involving teens 16 and older into the more than 7,000 annual domestic violence cases.

It's definitely prevalent. We sure see our share, Bridges said. Bridges said parents often call him saying, "I'm concerned about this guy my daughter is dating." But parents should get involved before it gets to that stage. "Intervene," Bridges said. Get her the help she needs to get out of the

I cringe at the thought of how many girls this must happen to every day without our noticing.

relationship. Or, if you suspect your son of abusing his girlfriend, enroll him in a Police Department, YWCA or Wichita Area Sexual Assault Center program, Bridges said.

Caring people did try to intervene for Raeshawnda. But suggestions were not enough. She and three of her friends died in the city's first quadruple homicide in 27 years. A jury convicted Raeshawnda's boyfriend, Cornelius Oliver, and sentenced him to life in prison for the crimes.

A case like Raeshawnda's hits us where we live. Not every boy abuses his date. But anyone with a daughter, or anyone who knows a teenage girl for that matter, has to feel a jolt at the thought of her with broken teeth and facial fractures or begging for her life with her back against a wall. You may not remember Raeshawnda Wheaton, but you should, particularly if you have a daughter with a boy-friend.

Her violent boyfriend eventually killed her.

PARENTING IS KEY TO CURBING GANG VIOLENCE

March 20, 2005

An open letter to permissive, uninvolved parents, specifically those of you with children in street gangs: I realize many of you didn't get to witness the melee at Towne East Square that police say 25 to 30 of your children were involved in last weekend, though you should have.

Wichita police said two gangs clashed at the mall's food court, scattering frightened shoppers while officers from the mall substation sprinted into the fray. Zales and Belden Jewelers closed as a precaution, and a crowd gathered to watch the fight from the balcony overhead.

Police arrested four of your children on misdemeanor battery charges. Another, bloodied in the fracas, went to a hospital. Your kiddos also shattered a pane of glass on the mall elevator. You should know that police say the free-for-all reflects rising tensions between street gangs over recent weeks—and offers a glimpse of what the city can expect as warm weather returns. "We didn't know a lot of them, and that's worrisome," Lt. J.T. Easter said of the young people involved in the fight. "We've got a lot of younger kids starting to get involved."

Easter says police are seeing the emergence of second- and third-generation gang members along with an influx of gang members returning from prison. The recent telltale signs of a gathering gang storm—more assaults, more drive-bys, and more confrontations between gangs— haven't been seen here since the early to mid-1990s.

Police say they have taken six guns off teen gang-bangers in the past week, bad news for a city trying to build economic momentum and attract new businesses. "We're not back there (the 1990s) by any means, but we're starting to see the same stuff," Easter said. "We're trying to get ahold of this now." Police said they plan to have an in-

But when your child touches off a skirmish and stampede, a lot of people, including me, need to get all up in your business.

creased presence at the mall during spring break this week.

I bet the merchants there can't wait to see your kids again. Easter says officers have been stumping all over town in recent weeks, offering parents like you tips on keeping kids out of gangs, and meeting with community groups such as the Wichita Ministerial League. But you, parents, are the most important of those groups, he said. I hope you're listening.

I've wondered what was going on in your head when you pulled up at school to drop off your children with songs such as 50 Cent's "Candy Shop" throbbing from the car speakers. The multiple-gunshot-victim-turned-rapper uses lollipops and other candy imagery to describe a kinky sexcapade.

I wonder what you're thinking when you dress your darling little girls like professional women and, by professional, I don't mean female executive. If I told you I objected to the raunchy music you allow your children to sing to and the raunchy clothes you put them in, you'd be within your rights to tell me to mind my own business.

But when your child touches off a skirmish and stampede, a lot of people, including me, need to get all up in your business. It's a miracle that more people weren't hurt in the mall fight. That with all of the people running, some child in a stroller wasn't trampled. Or, heaven forbid, that some little thug didn't pull out a gun and start firing into the crowd.

My first thought upon hearing about the disturbance was: How could children act this way without the parent knowing? Parents, you have to crack down on this kind of behavior for us to have a fighting chance at stopping the fighting. And if you don't, the rest of us will have to crack down on you. You may not have seen your children in action last weekend, but you certainly should have seen it coming.

DRAFT NEEDS PG RATING: CHILDREN SHOULDN'T WATCH NBA DRAFT

June 20, 2003

An old minister friend of mine lectured me once on the evils of the lottery. "It's a poor person's tax," he insisted, meaning that the people who could least afford to play it at all tended to play it the most—to their financial detriment.

And I don't think it is merely a coincidence that the first portion of the NBA draft is known as the "lottery." As is the case with its state-run counterpart, the NBA lottery is often watched by those who can least afford to.

Like some movies, it should get an R or at least a PG rating, not for violence or language but because children shouldn't watch it alone. Many of the little boys I talk to during the school year see a professional basketball career in their future. As a result, many of them shun schoolwork, convinced they won't need an education when they become millionaires.

Year-round league programs and summer camps designed to identify talent early have rubber-armed any leverage education may have held by requiring at least a C-average for eligibility.

Yes, indeed, "going pro" has become a child's version of his or her parent's Powerball aspirations, and the odds of winning aren't much different. Consider: Of the 540,000 athletes who make their high school basketball team, only 16,000 will play at NCAA colleges and universities. Of the 400 jobs in the NBA, only 60 or so open each year. And most of those who make the team will ride the bench.

Despite those statistics, fewer and fewer college players actually graduate, because the lure of millions seduces them into making the jump to the big leagues. This year's top draft choice, LeBron "King" James, considered leaving high school before he graduated in order to enter the NBA.

Of the 400 jobs in the NBA, only 60 or so open each year. And most of those who make the team will ride the bench.

But more often than not, that seduction ends with the suitors being stood up for their date with destiny.

Sportswriter Frank Deford said during a talk here in Wichita a few years ago that the nation's attitude toward sports has morphed for the worse. Once upon a time, he said, children were taught that it wasn't whether you win or lose, but how you play the game. Then the mantra became: "Winning isn't everything, it's the only thing." Today, "in your face" reigns as the sports world's guiding principle.

Maybe our values have crumbled along with our sense of sportsmanship. Scratching your way to success isn't the principled path we once insisted our children follow. Even I can remember being taught that anything worth having was worth working for. Instead, our materialism and permissive attitudes have actually taught this generation the opposite, namely: Anything worth having should come easy.

So if you love sports and you love kids, watch the draft with them next week. Talk to them about the hard work that goes into earning a spot on a team. Explain that they also should prepare academically for another career. And most important, let them know that they can scratch and win in life, without gambling with their future.

YOUNG BLACK MEN: HELP ME UNDERSTAND

April 20, 2006

A letter to young black men hurtling toward an early death: I read about yet another shooting this week. Easter morning, someone sprayed a 22-year-old with bullets, killing him in his front yard. The weekend before that, someone shot a 16-year-old in the head. Before that, two other young men died, only hours and maybe a mile apart, in separate drive-bys. That's why I'm writing you.

Each time I hear about another of these senseless shootings, it occurs to me that you're giving or taking away something that isn't even promised to you—your tomorrows. I need to know what's going on with you. I need you to explain it to me, because I can't call it. I'm pushing 40 now. I feel out of touch with what you believe, what you think, what you feel. I don't understand, so I need you to break it down for me.

Because I know that you're more than the turmoil in your life and the violent circumstances of your death.

Though I grew up in the same neighborhood where gunfire claps many nights, you probably don't think I could understand. I'm too old-school, too middle-class, too removed from the realities of your life. Mike Jones, I am not. But only time and a handful of personal decisions separate us. We really aren't that different.

Too many people are trying to talk for you. The conferences at big hotels where rich people get together to discuss your life are about the speakers at the conference. Not about you. You should know that I've heard tough talk my whole life. My Pops says he was "born in a cradle of butcher knives, rocked in a cradle of bee hives. Rattlesnakes bit me then crawled off and died."

But I also learned from him and from my mother that the toughest thing you'll do in life is persevere. Hold out hope when there's no reason to. Hold on. But so many of you seem to be giving up. Giving up on tomorrow.

Some of that is our fault. We have taken the fight out of people in your generation by making racism appear so insurmountable and omnipresent that some of you feel you have no alternative but to abandon tomorrow before it arrives. We adults haven't equipped you with the coping skills you need.

I do realize that a thug life serves a purpose for you, but I wonder if you've considered how choosing life in a gang also could mean that you're giving up on life. That you're saying to yourself, "I can't make it until tomorrow. I'm not strong enough to ride out this out." But I know you can. Anyone who chooses to face the possibility of uncertain death every day clearly has the personal courage to simply live. The Bible tells us we "are more than conquerors." Literally, that means that we are more than a match for whatever challenge we face in life.

That's why I ache so when I read about yet another one of you dying. Because you deserve better. Because I know that you're more than the turmoil in your life and the violent circumstances of your death. Because I have love for you. And this ain't no surface love. It's deep. I see myself in you, and I see you in all of the stand-up black men who have helped me. I see your potential to someday help someone else.

It may all sound a little too simple: We talk, you change your life. I'll admit that. But I can't just sit around watching the body count mount and wish I had said something. A little caring, a little guidance and a little love went a long way in my life.

So write me. E-mail me. Call me and we'll set up a meeting. Anything. Easter has passed, but God says your chance for redemption hasn't. I want to understand. And then I want you to understand how important your tomorrow is. Maybe you can be convinced to hang on long enough to actually see yours.

Your brother in the struggle, Mark

BOYFRIENDS, BABIES OFTEN MIX POORLY

February 19, 2006

A 3-year-old boy held in scalding water is being treated for third-degree burns at the Via Christi Regional Medical Center-St. Francis Campus. His mother, 23-year-old Amber K. Pierce, and her boyfriend, 24-year-old Rex L. Wells III, have been charged with felony child abuse for the incident authorities say happened about a week ago.

Friday, an ll-month-old boy died from head injuries doctors said don't appear accidental. Police have booked the boyfriend of the child's aunt on charges of first-degree murder. A charge isn't a conviction. There's a lot to sort through yet. We don't know much about the dynamics of these relationships.

Still, the circumstances surrounding these cases ring sadly familiar to prosecutors. Many—if not most—of the 1,800 abuse or molestation cases affecting 2,500 children each year in Sedgwick County involve a mother's or a caretaker's boyfriend, said District Attorney Nola Foulston. "This is a constant thorn in my side," she said.

How many abuse cases could we eliminate if mothers had an option other than moving in with a boyfriend? If they wouldn't be homeless otherwise? If they weren't dependent on the boyfriend for support? "A significant amount," Foulston said. "Anecdotally, obviously, it would have a dramatic impact."

In the past two years, other cases involving abusive boyfriends have made headlines: Police arrested a 20-year-old man for the beating of his girlfriend's 2-year-old. A 3-month-old died after her mother's boyfriend shook and bit her to death.

Boyfriends often find a child extraneous to their relationship with a woman, a competitor for her attention, Foulston said. "There's a lack of bonding there along with a

The mothers often insist that they've shielded children from the sounds in another room. But the kids know.

lack of understanding and maturity," she said. "They don't understand a baby's cry and they end up hurting the baby because it won't stop crying."

A power differential, in which a mother comes to rely on a boyfriend financially, makes the situation worse. "These girls can't do it on their own, and they get hooked up with the wrong people," Foulston said. "They put the relationship ahead of their kids."

The boyfriend also may be abusing the mother, said Fran Betzen Cook, staff supervisor at Harbor House, a domestic violence shelter. Many women with sons remain with abusive boyfriends because they think their sons need male role models, Cook said.

The mothers often insist that they've shielded children from the sounds in another room. But the kids know. And half the time when the mother is being abused, so are the children, Cook said. "What they don't realize is that sometimes the boyfriend will start hurting the mom first and once he has her under control, they can more easily hurt the children," she said. A lot of the women know they're between a rock and a hard place but without a job that pays a living wage, surviving as a single parent can feel impossible.

"It's really frustrating when they go back to an abuser for financial reasons," Cook said. That's why Cook says more beds are needed in the emergency shelter. So are more donations to help women with kids go to school, find jobs and find safe, affordable housing.

The problem is larger than you might think. Last year, Harbor House had to turn away 547 women. I shudder at the thought of how many were mothers who ended up at a boyfriend's house.

MOMS' LOW SELF-ESTEEM PUTS KIDS IN DANGER*

December 7, 2008

Go down the list of Wichita child homicide victims, and the person alone with the child at the time frequently reads: Boyfriend. Stepfather. Boyfriend. Boyfriend.

More often than not, the mothers haven't asked about or have ignored the criminal records of the men they left alone with their children. Isn't this yet another bit of evidence that people are so starved for intimacy, they're willing to place themselves and even their children in harm's way? District Attorney Nola Foulston has railed about this problem for years.

You might think it's about women avoiding homelessness and depending on men they barely know. That it's about day care. Or about women falling for men who view her children as rivals for her attention.

Karen King, a social worker assigned to Wesley Hospital's pediatric intensive care unit, says it's deeper than that. The Department of Social and Rehabilitative Services will pay for child care, rent and food, King said.

It's really about the mother's low self-esteem, and she says she sees the horrific results nearly every day. It isn't uncommon, she says, for mothers to bring small children to the hospital and barely visit them. She's had to call them and ask, "Are you visiting your child today?" The mothers tell her things like they're going out for their birthday.

"Can you imagine how frightening it must be for a child to be in a hospital with no one around they know? No one to sit with them or rock them?" King said.

King said she reached one such parent as a child lay on a gurney heading into surgery. The mother needed to come in to sign permission waivers. "She said she couldn't come in," King recalled, "because her cat had been picked up the previous day and she needed to bail him out."

Take a school child balloons or cupcakes on his or her birthday if that child has a parent who can't or won't.

But you don't have to be a social worker to see such things. Visit a school or talk to a teacher. You'll learn about the hungry kids who come to school in dirty clothes. Kids so starved of care and direction at home that they don't know how to accept unconditional love and attack the people at school who offer it. And you'll learn how those kids burn out young teachers who earnestly believe that if they just loved these kids enough, they could help them.

The kids are products of our culture of indifference that values things over people. So many people treat relationships as transactions: something simple and immediate. Then wonder why those relationships seem so fleeting, superficial and empty.

If you are a woman trapped in such a place right now, please get help. Go to a church—any church. Call the Wichita Women's Initiative Network. Call me. I'll find help for you.

The rest of us need to learn how to give back, King said. Along the way, maybe we can teach children about how relationships need time to develop. Perhaps when they grow up, they'll make better choices for themselves and their children.

Take a school child balloons or cupcakes on his or her birthday if that child has a parent who can't or won't. Imagine what it must be like when all of the kids around you get birthday treats and you realize that may never happen on your birthday.

Pay the fee for a child to play Biddy Basketball. King says when she's in line at a store and sees a mother struggling with a child, she asks, "May I hold the baby while you write the check?" She uses those moments to offer the only encouragement the child may get that day.

Sneering at self-esteem efforts has become chic. And maybe some efforts to raise kids' self-esteem do go too far. But go down that list of children—babies—who died this year in Wichita in no small part because their parent was dying for love. Then tell me self-esteem isn't important.

TODAY'S GANG CULTURE IS NEW FORM OF SLAVERY

May 23, 2010

If you haven't seen the Slavery 3.0 program yet, the new application will amaze you. Gangs have streamlined the design since the 1.0 version with its whips, chains and overpacked ships. It also surpasses the 2.0, sharecropping version, which featured clever accounting and fuzzy math.

This version, also known as "gang culture," operates more efficiently. No embarrassing three-fifths compromises or US Supreme Court references to Dred Scott. You get the psychological, spiritual, social and physical devastation, without the worrisome guilt and direct-control bondage. No muss, no fuss. Just sit back and watch this program work.

Slavery 3.0 organizes subjects into warring factions leading primarily to incarceration. Felonies lock the incarcerated out of the economy, so they work for free as more morally tolerant captives of the multiplatform, for-profit, prison industrial complex. Franchising offers endless opportunities. Most gang culture growth in the past 20 years gained traction in small-to-midsize markets.

Karen Countryman-Roswurm, a doctoral student who works with the sexually exploited, says the program spawned another form of slavery. Countryman-Roswurm and police say gangs snatch children, hook them on drugs and force them into Internet porn and sex slavery.

Unlike the mortgage bubble, this one won't burst. Why? Volume. We have more than 2 million people in prison, about 46 percent of them African Americans. How many sons or nephews have they placed on the prison-conveyor belt on their way there?

Consider the growth potential. The black population accounts for 12 percent of the US population. But only a sliver of that percentage accounts for that 46 percent after controlling for the young, the old and the law-abiding. Slavery 3.0 has inventory to burn.

The Pied Piper entertainment industry offers around-the-clock tech support and free advertising. It reinforces gang culture's core value of hedonism. Vulnerable children sleepwalk toward this program like sagging-jeaned zombies.

Gang culture will outperform any other investment for decades. Ron Matson, chairman of Wichita State University's sociology department, says gang culture indicts society's unwillingness to allow swaths of its culture to fully participate.

"When we all have access to a legitimate economy that works well for everyone, there will be less need for gangs to solve problems relating to poverty, under-education and discrimination," Matson said.

Don't count on this anytime soon, though. The federal Centers for Disease Control and Prevention said only last year that homicide represented the leading cause of death for African American Kansans ages 10 to 24. That is Slavery 3.0's genius. It gets its target audience to participate in its own destruction.

So saddle up, entrepreneurs, for the gold-tooth, gold rush. And don't worry about your investments running off. They punish their own for upward aspirations. They call it "acting white."

You can find Slavery 3.0 at convenient, street-corner locations near you. Don't hurry. Supplies seem unlimited.

MICHAEL VICK: CHARACTER VS. CONSEQUENCE

August 23, 2007

So you like Atlanta Falcon quarterback Michael Vick? Think he's cool? Like the style, the swagger? How do you like him now? Were you crushed when he announced Monday he plans to plead guilty to federal dog-fighting charges? I wasn't.

In fact, I thought it might turn out to be a good thing for kids to learn how expensive cool can be. Why? The symbolism of Vick's fall is worth more than a lifetime of public service announcements. Kids who want to emulate his swagger should see this collapse for what it is—a lesson of how values do matter.

I don't know Michael Vick and can't vouch for his character. But given his recent troubles, his life appeared to be out of control. In the past couple of years, Vick allegedly used the alias Ron Mexico in seeking diagnosis or treatment for an STD. He waved the wrong finger at fans and tried to get a water bottle with a false bottom through airport security and was suspected of smoking marijuana. He was vindicated of the marijuana accusations. But how much does that matter now?

Nike pulled its endorsement deal. Reebok stopped selling Vick's jersey. Two companies and counting have dropped his trading card. The Falcons may insist that he repay upwards of $20 million of his $37 million signing bonus. And, of course, now he probably has a sizable lawyer bill. Pretty cool, huh?

As part of the deal struck with federal prosecutors, Vick will plead guilty to felony charges of conspiring to travel in interstate commerce in aid of unlawful activities and conspiring to sponsor a dog in an animal-fighting venture. He faces a year in prison, the loss of millions in future en-

Vick created his own problems by indulging in this disgusting practice, but they were compounded by the crew he ran with, some of them family.

dorsements, the loss of a $130 million NFL contract and possibly the end of his career.

All because he wanted to watch dogs kill each other. Vick created his own problems by indulging in this disgusting practice, but they were compounded by the crew he ran with, some of them family.

Police stumbled onto Vick's dog-fighting enterprise after the April 20 arrest of his cousin, Davon Boddie. A drug dog alerted its handler to a marijuana scent in Boddie's vehicle; he now faces possession and intent to distribute charges. Police then raided a Vick-owned property where Boddie lived, looking for drugs, and found dog-fighting evidence.

I was a Michael Vick fan. You needed a seat belt just to watch this man compete. He's the only player to run as well as pass for 1,000 yards in a season.

But as dangerous as he may have been on the field, he could be more effective off it in making the connection between character and consequence for young people. We have a generation of youth seemingly obsessed with avoiding pretense but adhering to one big pretense of hollow machismo and shallow, consumer-driven self-esteem. Kids are missing the link between character and consequence.

Perhaps from his cell, in prison-issue clothing, having lost a sports empire and its fortune, Vick can help shatter the image of ignorance that many young people seem so wrapped up in. That would be so cool.

I'm Sorry, But I Won't Enable You Anymore

August 5, 2005

I'm this close to leaving you. This relationship isn't working. A lot of us middle-class and working class black folks aren't sure how things got so bad between us and you —our brothers and sisters mired in hopelessness and help-lessness. Those falling further and further behind. Those I don't seem to know anymore.

I love you. I always will. But I have to love you enough to tell you the truth.

You have to stop living in the past. You're still marching and pointing fingers at white people the way you did in 1963 and expecting the same results.

I wonder, were we together then, or did we just have the same enemy? When that part of the movement died, you went your way and I went mine. We ended up here, with so much hurt between us that I wonder if we'll ever be the same.

We don't talk much anymore, and when we do, we argue. We have almost nothing in common. You won't listen to anyone. People have tried to tell you some of this, but you got angry. No, maybe they weren't nice about it, but they were right. We do need some community behavior standards.

I know I can be self-important and saditty. I know I throw my success in your face. I'm sorry. That's wrong. I should view my accomplishments as something that can make me a better friend. But nothing is ever your fault. It's always me or "the system" holding you down. You're too easily offended and unnecessarily confrontational.

You ridicule me for trying to live better, for trying to learn. You ask me, "How does Uncle Tom's cabin look on the inside?" Yet you still expect me to fetch and carry for you. I get up and bust my butt at work or at school or at

I remember when about all that sustained us was the love we had for one another. It really felt like us against the world.

137

both every day, and when I get home, you're still on the corner or on the couch with a new excuse as to why you can't work.

Do you really think I face a racism-free world? I don't, but I face it. It is bad sometimes, but nothing close to what our parents and grandparents faced. You have to summon the courage to try and to fail and to accept responsibility for all of it. And then try again. But it doesn't appear that you're even trying to change.

Look at what you're doing to the kids. They're out of control. They're joining gangs, shooting at each other, marking up their bodies, wearing their pants below their butts (boys and girls), speaking at best a variant of English. And then you blame the schools, the ministers, everyone —everyone but you.

And this seductive hip-hop hoochie they're always with fills their heads with shallow, ignorant and profane images. They need to drop her like she's hot.

The kids aren't bad. They've just never had anyone love them, teach them or put them first. The streets and the prisons dine sumptuously on them daily. For this and for other reasons, white flight from neighborhoods isn't just white anymore. Today, the races have come together, if only to flee uncivil behavior.

It's difficult to face what you and I have become. I remember when about all that sustained us was the love we had for one another. It really felt like us against the world. You used to talk about us learning to run uphill so that if the ground ever leveled, we'd be stronger and faster. That's how I so fondly remember you. Strong. Funny. Generous. Smart. Creative. Industrious. Warm.

I know what I'm saying sounds harsh, but I've got to know: Do you want this relationship? I do. I'm this close to leaving, but I haven't. I'm here for you if you want to change, but I won't enable you anymore. Maybe the second time around, we'll get what we wanted and save what we had. For your sake and for ours, I hope you decide soon. I won't wait forever.

ALI: SPEAKING TO A LOSS SHARED BY MANY

September 21, 2016

Muhammad Ali often made surprise elementary school visits in Louisville, Kentucky, his hometown and where I began my journalism career. One such visit at his niece's school prompted a hasty assembly.

"Who's the baddest kid in the school?" the Champ rasped, biting his bottom lip, settling into a boxing stance and stirring the air with his fists. In unison, the children pointed to a boy seated next to his teacher. Ali waved him down from the bleachers to the floor for some playful shadowboxing.

As the Saturday reporter, I got the scoop. The Champ baked the boy a cake.

But one of the first things you immediately notice about Ali is his size. When he snatched the heavyweight title from Sonny Liston in 1964, Liston had to look up at the 22-year-old challenger in the center of the ring before the fight and got acquainted with the young man's ham-sized fists.

If Ali loomed large physically and figuratively to adults, he looked like a mountain to that child. With a slight Ali feint, the frightened boy bounded back up the bleachers and into his teacher's lap. Ali, we were told at the newspaper, felt terrible and later asked the teacher about the boy. She told Ali that the boy was fine and was about a day away from his birthday. Ali reflexively invited the boy and a couple of friends to his mother's home for a private party.

As the Saturday reporter, I got the scoop. The Champ baked the boy a cake. He magically pulled quarters and ribbons from his ears and in a grand finale, stood in front of us and appeared to levitate.

As the boys and the teacher later filed out of the house buzzing, he extended his hand and as I shook it, he brushed my cheek with his and said "Asalam Alaikum." When I returned the greeting, "Walaikum Salam," he seemed stunned. "Are you a Muslim, brother?" "No, but I know about the greeting," I said. "Wait here," he said, and disappeared down a hallway. He returned with a Koran and a Bible. He sat me down and for about an hour, pointed out numerical discrepancies between Bible passages. A first reference to an assembled army might say 5,000 soldiers while a subsequent reference would say 50,000.

Then he asked why Christians tampered with the Bible so much. A King James Version. A New King James Version. A Good News Bible. A New International Version. This is the foundation of your faith, he said, and you alter it several times a year? "The Koran is the same today as it was when Muhammad brought it down from the mountain," he said. This had never occurred to me. It felt profound. He seemed so sincere.

Since his death, I've noticed how so many people have a photo with the Champ or a story about meeting him.

I eventually lifted my journalistic mask and told him he had long been my hero and that I would appreciate this meeting for the rest of my life. I added that while everything he'd taught me felt compelling, I wouldn't be converting to Islam.

He smiled. I told him I needed to go because I was the only reporter working that day. I wanted desperately to beg for an autograph, but couldn't bring myself to do it. As I stood up though, he reached into a long box of his boxing trading cards. He signed two of them, folded his handwritten list of Bible verses he'd scribbled for me to study around them, and handed the entire trove to me.

Since his death, I've noticed how so many people have a photo with the Champ or a story about meeting him. It has kind of lost its cachet. But I will of course cherish my story because its symmetry seemed to so perfectly align with the arc of his life. The shadowboxing and playful overbite. Drawing people to him. Baking a cake for a child he'd accidentally frightened. Throwing a private birthday party. Performing a magic show.

And then, in the quiet of his mother's dining room, he takes the time to share the wonders of his faith with a stranger and then cares enough to send him off with a most cherished gift.

Ali gave the world so much. It's no wonder so many of us—the once-frightened boy, me and a billion others—feel such a tremendous loss in his passing.

WHETHER YOU LIKE ICE-T OR NOT, 'IT HAPPENS'

July 26, 1992

It happens. The red and blue lights were flashing and the officer was telling me through the speaker on top of the cruiser to stop and put my hands on my head.

I was 15, on a bicycle, barely 100 pounds and in front of my house about to turn into my driveway. He said nothing more until he pulled me off the bicycle by the back of my neck, squeezing with a sandpaper grip. He reeked of intimidation. Embarrassing stares from onlookers tightened around me. My face was like a clenched fist. "I live right here in this house, could I push my bike into the yard?"

"Leave it in the street," he said. The officer swung a pair of handcuffs from his holster and slapped them on my wrists.

"What did I do?"

"Quiet, please," and he tightened them as I winced.

As the cruiser rolled away, I yelled to a friend of our family, to tell my mother that I was being taken away, but didn't know where. I was never read my rights. It happens, even in Wichita, Kansas.

The Dog and Shake, a hamburger restaurant about eight blocks away had been robbed and a couple of its workers had a knife held to their throats. I was the suspect. I felt the sandpaper on my arm as he pulled me from the car at the restaurant.

One of the workers shook with frustration as we approached. She said she couldn't believe that after she spent those horrible seconds with death resting on her chin that the officer could return with this "child." "Look at him, he can't be more than 14," she said crying. "Let that child go."

The sandpaper was back on my neck and we were in the cruiser and around the corner as my mother screeched into the parking lot. She ran out seconds later in a panic. "Oh

One of the workers shook with frustration as we approached. . .

142

my God, they got my baby."

It happens. But it probably won't happen to George Bush, Dan Quayle or any of the other socially advantaged men boycotting rapper Ice-T's album *Body Count,* with its controversial single, "Cop Killer." I doubt any of them would be treated so roughly and disrespectfully. Or stopped at all for that matter. I doubt any of them would have to worry about themselves or their sons being bludgeoned with nightsticks and drilled with taser darts in a flood of headlights.

The lyrics of "Cop Killer" are crude but derived from the vulgar realities Ice-T witnessed as a youngster in South Central Los Angeles.

The majority of officers who have stopped me have been firm but fair, either efficiently issuing the citation or sending me off with a warning. Yet it's difficult to move beyond being torn from my bicycle seat and looking into blue eyes filled with irrational anger. It's difficult to move beyond the times I've been stopped and asked if my car was mine, where I was going and told to "just watch it."

. . . She said she couldn't believe that after she spent those horrible seconds with death resting on her chin that the officer could return with this "child."

It happens. It happened in Belleville, Illinois, where *The Belleville News Democrat* reported two years ago that the chief of police formed a special unit to stop, ticket and harass black motorists in West Belleville, which borders predominantly black East St. Louis.

"This was a way Chief (Robert) Hurst had, he thought, to legally intimidate and harass black people for all to see and (have them) go back and tell their friends, 'You better not go to Belleville or they'll stop you,'" said Timothy Roeper, a Belleville patrolman from 1984 to 1990.

It happened in Teaneck, New Jersey, where a 16-year-old boy was shot, apparently while his hands were raised. It happened in Los Angeles after the rioting when an autopsy found that a 15-year-old boy killed by sheriff's deputies had been shot in the back.

It happened in Rochester Hills, Michigan, a Detroit suburb when my best friend, Lions all-pro running back Barry Sanders, and I were stopped in a parking lot for driving too cautiously, for too long, too late at night in too nice a car in too nice a neighborhood.

It even happens here [Louisville, Kentucky]. Jefferson County police officer Larry Bush shot John Lewis, a fleeing 17-year-old Newburg youth, after failing to chase him down during a robbery stakeout in 1989. Fred Douglas Randolph Jr. told *The Courier-Journal* that he's been stopped nine times as a result of an intensified community policing effort seeking to crack down on crime in housing projects.

Sarah Smith, who lives at the Parkhill housing project, said she and dozens of other residents watched as police threw a suspect to the ground, "had the billy bats across his neck. He was handcuffed. Then they hit him with the flashlights. They drug him on out and put him in the car."

But the privileged and pompous voices of Bush, Quayle, Alabama Governor Guy Hunt and others who will never have to fear for their lives from police officers would rather condemn Ice-T, who speaks to the hurt and rage of urban youth all over the country, than deal with the real problem. It's easier to accuse Time Warner Inc. [Ice-T's label] of marketing "murder for money" than to do what Walt Tangel and others in the Jefferson County Police department's community foot patrols program are attempting to accomplish—beating the streets instead of people and trying to close that vast racial schism.

Bush and others would rather pull a record off the shelf and squelch the voice that is actually warning police of a potential explosion of violence unless they bring their nightsticks under control.

Those law enforcement groups shouting down Ice-T would do well to follow the lead of the 35,000-member National Black Police Association, which says it will not join the boycott. "Where were these police groups when the police beat up Rodney King?" asked Ronald Hampton, the group's executive director. "Why were they not appalled by the actions of their brothers? It rings of hypocrisy."

I could barely get my mother to talk about the incident or the Ice-T controversy. From her world of country music —Kenny Rogers and Conway Twitty—she says she can't

> *I could barely get my mother to talk about the incident or the Ice-T controversy.*

relate to the jarring, often discordant street drama Ice-T conjures with his music. The memory is still painful. But I'm 24 now, and I can still remember the anger in her eyes as she yelled at the policeman who brought me home and the fear in her eyes each time I left the house at night on an errand or with friends. I know on some level she can relate to Ice-T's rage.

It happens, Mr. Bush, but it probably wouldn't happen to you.

THE BLACK BRAIN DRAIN

March 8, 1997

. . . the irony of the situation is that Kansas is so much a part of the history of black people— from John Brown's fights against slavery to the Brown v. Topeka Board of Education ruling on school desegregation.

Many of the houses in the neighborhood where Charles McAfee grew up near Ninth Street and Cleveland now sag with age. Some are rickety; others are boarded up. It isn't the neighborhood McAfee remembers. He grew up in a neighborhood of close-knit families who wanted their children to get ahead through education—a neighborhood that produced about 15 children who, McAfee says, went on to receive doctorates.

Those children are gone now, along with their advanced degrees. Their departure is just one example of what some community and education officials call a "black brain drain" that, little by little, has hurt Wichita and its surrounding communities.

Those officials said the loss of such talented people has robbed young people—black and white—of important role models, and it has robbed the community of civic leadership.

"I've always had a positive attitude about the changes we could make in Wichita," said McAfee, an internationally respected architect. "I wouldn't be here if I still didn't have some hope. But Wichita has no excuse not to have had a black president of a major corporation or a black superintendent of schools or someone in City Hall in a major position of importance. This doesn't make sense. There are too many talented people who have come through this town."

Much of the problem has to do with the economic profile of the city. David Wright, assistant professor of sociology at Wichita State University, said the Wichita market is known for its strong blue-collar work force, but that means white-collar workers—black or white—often leave. Because the black pool is smaller, the loss seems greater.

A study by *The Wichita Eagle* more than 10 years ago

146

found that nearly 60 percent of Kansas high school students who were National Merit semifinalists from 1970 to 1980 were living, working or studying outside the state.

That study claimed that the main culprit behind the brain drain was the state's failure to meet the work needs of skilled and highly educated Kansans. It also showed that many people perceive Kansas as too quiet, too rural and overly wholesome—no place for a bright young person enamored of cultural activities, diversity in entertainment and cuisine, and urban excitement.

Many of the findings of the study still seem relevant today. Black white-collar workers have an added burden: the legacy of institutional racism in the city, and the persistent sense that there are limited opportunities for advancement and success. Talk to black Wichitans coming out of college, and they will say they simply don't see many black people in the kinds of positions they would ultimately like to hold.

In the school system, in the government and in the business community, there are not many black managers or executives. Only six of the 830 doctors listed as members of the Medical Society of Sedgwick County are black, and only two of them are family doctors. None of the major law firms in Wichita has a black associate or partner, said Sedgwick County District Court Judge Gregory Waller. Few black people have ever been named to judgeships in Kansas, and no black person has ever sat on the Kansas Supreme Court.

As for the media that cover the market, *The Wichita Eagle* has one black manager and two black journalists; the three local television stations have a few black people behind the cameras and just one black on-air personality; and the many radio stations in town have a handful of black employees.

Obviously, there is no way to account for every professional field, just as there is no way to quantify how much of a brain drain has occurred. The state's colleges and universities don't keep comprehensive numbers on where students go after graduation. The individual professional schools that do keep numbers don't separate them by race. It is fair to note that although many black professionals leave Wichita, others come here for work, particularly as engineers in the aircraft industry.

About 11 percent of the Wichita population is black, as is about 9 percent of the Sedgwick County population. The suburban numbers are much smaller, but in general, the black population is slowly rising. Still, black professionals recount story after story of talented colleagues who pulled up stakes looking for opportunities they couldn't find here.

McAfee's family is a good example. His daughter, Cheryl McAfee—also an architect—has a master's degree from Harvard University. In the seven years after her graduation, the biggest project she could land in Wichita was a firehouse. She finally headed to Atlanta, where she landed a multi-million-dollar contract to manage the construction of all 35 venues for the 1996 Olympics.

McAfee's sister Gwen, now retired, struggled to build a medical career in Wichita. She ended up heading the hematology outpatient clinic at the UCLA Medical School in Los Angeles. McAfee himself has difficulty finding work in Wichita; he continues to be based here, but his biggest projects have been elsewhere.

"It's not important just for African American kids to see African American professionals," Chandler said...

"The city's profile would be so much higher and the respect for the city would be so much higher," McAfee said. "And this town would have been hard pressed to have kept all of us in line or down for so long."

Ron Walters said he found few opportunities as a student at WSU in the 1960s, so he transferred to Fisk University in Tennessee, a historically black school. He went on to become chairman of the political science department at Howard University in Washington, D.C., and chief campaign strategist for two of the Rev. Jesse Jackson's presidential campaigns. He is now a professor at the University of Maryland. He has never worked in Wichita.

"It has always been extremely difficult for people to break into professional roles," Walters said. "It has been a perennial war for years."

John Gaston, head of the department of Communication Arts at Valdosta State University in Georgia, said the irony of the situation is that Kansas is so much a part of the history of black people—from John Brown's fights against slavery to the *Brown v. Topeka Board of Education* ruling on school desegregation.

Gaston taught at WSU for nearly 20 years but left in 1992 when he felt he had hit a professional dead end. "It's the perception that what we (black people) do doesn't contribute to what is important," Gaston said. "Wichita needs to understand how what we have to offer fits into the big picture."

One example often cited in the black community is the treatment of Gordon Parks, a world-famous photographer, writer and filmmaker born in Fort Scott. Some of Parks' photos were put on display a few years ago at WSU's Edwin A. Ulrich Museum. Parks thought the museum would keep them as part of its permanent collection. However, WSU returned the photos to him, saying there was no room to store them. In a letter to *The Eagle* in 1995, Parks said he was told in no uncertain terms that "the Ulrich no longer wanted the collection."

Elizabeth King, who oversees the Ulrich Museum, said it shipped the collection back to Parks because it did not believe it owned the pieces. Nevertheless, other museums around the country had been vying for the collection, and the perception—right or wrong—was that WSU had pushed it away. Ultimately, the Corcoran Gallery in Washington, D.C., received a million dollar grant from the Ford Motor Company to continue showing and building the exhibit.

Anna Chandler, assistant professor and program director at WSU's Hugo Wall School of Urban and Public Affairs, said the black brain drain—and the negative perceptions that accompany it—translates into a loss of economic power, leadership and role models for children.

"It's not important just for African American kids to see African American professionals," Chandler said. "White children need to see them, too, to get a realistic view of what America is about."

Jim Rhatigan, vice president of student affairs at WSU,

". . . White children need to see them, too, to get a realistic view of what America is about."

said cities must dismantle barriers that keep people from reaching their potential. "This is not just a theoretical good idea," Rhatigan said. "This is a very practical reality. The cities that do this will prosper and the ones that don't, won't. Human potential is not confined to one race."

Chirpy Fields is an example of the kind of "human potential" Rhatigan was talking about. Fields graduated last year from Columbia University in New York with a master's degree in education. She wanted to work in Wichita, where she grew up and where her family still lives. But the only job she could get was as a temporary secretary. Now she is pursuing a career as an administrator back in New York.

Too often, McCray said, parents remember the segregated Wichita they grew up in . . .

"There are so few games in town that when you get kicked off the field, you still can't get into another game, even if you have your own bat and ball," she said. "I'm sitting there thinking, 'I have an Ivy League degree, and here I am, a secretary.' " Experiences like Fields' only serve to reinforce perceptions in the black community about the problems they face in the Wichita area.

How is it that people who are "unqualified" in Wichita can go to other cities and excel? What is it about Wichita that makes it seem inhospitable to black professionals? Most important, what can be done to improve the situation so the community can benefit from its homegrown talent?

Most observers say some of the answers can come from innovative programs that encourage young people to remain in the community. The "Grow Your Own Teacher" program operated by the Wichita school district is one example.

The program pays the college tuition of minority Wichitans who want to become teachers. Those teachers must return to Wichita classrooms after graduation and pay back the school district by teaching for a few years.

Sam Spaght, assistant superintendent for curriculum delivery for the school district, said 42 of the 49 teachers who have gone through the program are now teaching in Wichita schools.

The legal community is making a similar effort. Terry

Unruh, an attorney with Grace, Unruh and Pratt, said the Wichita Bar Association has started a Grow Your Own Lawyer program in an attempt to encourage minority high school students to consider legal careers. The 10 high school seniors in the program have been paired with lawyers who will try to mentor the students through college and law school, Unruh said.

Nevertheless, Sharon Cranford, who operates perhaps the state's largest annual minority college fair, said schools must boost the number of scholarships offered to black students with good high school academic records. "If they are not athletes, I don't see that colleges are very interested," Cranford said.

And Orin Boyd, Jr., a Wichita native who is now director of business development for a Baltimore credit card processing company, said Wichita also needs to start aggressively seeking businesses that offer opportunities to black professionals.

"Most of the friends and people I grew up with are in other cities looking for opportunities that don't exist in Wichita," Boyd said. "The $50,000-, $60,000- and $70,000-a-year jobs just aren't there. If you invest in a college degree, where do you go to have a realistic opportunity for a six-figure salary?"

Former County Commissioner Billy McCray said some of the answers must come from the black community itself. Too often, McCray said, parents remember the segregated Wichita they grew up in and—directly or indirectly—send messages to their children that Wichita has no place for them.

McCray said black parents should rein in their frustrations and encourage their children to stay and contribute to the community. "You can't drive out all of the talented young people and expect to progress," McCray said.

Back in Charles McAfee's old neighborhood, a few new homes are going up. McAfee's company is building them. He's trying to help create a new neighborhood, a place where young people in close-knit families can grow up and get educated. Perhaps this time, they will stay around.

and—directly or indirectly—send messages to their children that Wichita has no place for them.

[Note: Wichita now has several black law partners, a black federal magistrate, and a black school superintendent, as well as having had a black mayor, police chief and fire chief since this story ran.]

OUR MUSLIM NEIGHBORS

February 14, 2017

I'm reminded sometimes of my most terrifying moment, by a smile.

It's almost always at Sam's Club, where I must shop in order to feed my now 12-year-old twins Mason and Morgan and two other sons. That's where I see Dr. Mohammed Ansari, the neonatal intensive care doctor who watched over the twins when they arrived weeks early. He sees me, and smiles.

I always shake his hand and thank him and frankly, he really does seem over it. My gushing seems to embarrass him. He'd merely done what his training dictated. He reacts as though I'm over thanking him.

. . . on the verge of violating tenets we claim to hold so dear, I fear for them and for us.

But I look at my twins today, with their mother's nose and my grandfather's long legs and my mother's intellect and think to myself that Dr. Ansari is lucky he's not at this moment wrapped in a bear-hug.

Dr. Ansari should know that I pray for his safety, too. In the current political climate aimed clumsily at Muslim people, I seethe at the fearfulness driving our public conversations and continue to hope we find the love and courage to govern our fears rather than capitulating to them.

I've not discussed his faith with him and the hospital website says he hails from Bangladesh, but that doesn't seem to matter much. The order meant to block people from certain countries doesn't seem too focused either and a federal court, in rescinding it, has said so. I understand fears of terrorism, but it's our response to it that makes all of the difference. As I said, I've known fear, too.

My wife spent several weeks on hospital bed rest trying to carry Mason and Morgan to term in a difficult pregnancy and on a hot August evening, Mason, "Baby A," entered the world with a wail. I waited for Morgan's, "Baby B's" voice, but he never cried. I followed them, my throat closing and my heart thudding, as they carried him out of the room, arms and legs dangling, and into the "NICU," or the neonatal intensive care unit. After a day or so, Mason joined him there as his temperature continued to drop.

We were there several times a night, changing tiny diapers and trying to get them to drink a mere ounce of formula. Their suckle instinct hadn't quite developed and I had to gently lift their chins and pull their cheeks forward to help them drink.

I remember a particular night when they simply wouldn't eat and my fears multiplied on my face. Dr. Ansari appeared. He smiled and reassured me. Put his hand on my shoulder. He told me that at 4 pounds each, they were the biggest babies in the unit. "They're going to be fine."

I've never forgotten those midnight and 4 a.m. moments. Or him. And in these moments of crisis, I think about the people like him who give so much.

Mason and Morgan McCormick.
Courtesy Mark McCormick.

I think about my good friend Abdul Arif who launched the Mayflower Clinic—a medical clinic staffed by immigrant doctors who wanted people to know that immigrants do actually contribute to American society. I think about Maurice El Hajj, the expert and kind-hearted mechanic who used to work on my car.

Even my East Wichita next door neighbors who, with smiles framed by a hijab, brought me bread when we moved in. They have each been so kind and so generous and work so hard to generate good will. I cringe at the thought that there are so many people unable to see through their skin or their culture or their religion and see their full humanity.

And in these dark moments for our country, on the verge of violating tenets we claim to hold so dear, I fear for them and for us. Fear can distort our perceptions in horrible ways. My own faith says love casts out fear and there's a dimension of love that needs to surface here. Violence is a reaction, a reflex. Peace is a choice.

Justice is the public face of love. There can be no love without justice. Our response to fear is key. I choose to smile.

I cringe at the thought that there are so many people unable to see through their skin or their culture or their religion and see their full humanity.

ABOUT THE AUTHOR

In 14 years at *The Wichita Eagle* Mark McCormick received more than 20 journalism and civic awards including three Gold Medals in five years from the Kansas City Press Club, a First Place Award in 2009 from the Kansas Press Association and a "Man of the Year" Award from Wichita Business and Professional Women.

Mark worked with football great Barry Sanders on Sanders' *New York Times* best-selling biography, *Barry Sanders: Now You See Him* (2003), and is featured in the journalism textbook, *Writing and Reporting News: a Coaching Method* by Carole Rich which is into its 7th edition. He's also a trustee at the William Allen White School of Journalism and Mass Communications.

Today, Mark is the executive director of The Kansas African American Museum (TKAAM) in Wichita and serves as a national board member of the Association of African American Museums (AAAM). He also spent nearly three years as Director of Communications at The Kansas Leadership Center.